Up Gently

GW00566686

Capt John Sutherland

SunRise

SunRise

First published in Great Britain in 2023 by SunRise

SunRise
A Division of Upper Octave Ltd
124 City Road
London EC1V 2NX

ISBN 978-1-9144894-2-6

A CIP catalogue record for this book is available from the
British Library.

Typeset in Georgia and Impact.

To the memory of Dick, Archie, Mike, John, Dick, Steve, Al, Roy, Mohammed, Graham, Norman, Steve, Brian and Pete.

They strapped in but never unstrapped.

John Sutherland

'The helicopter is closest to fulfilment of mankind's ancient dreams: the flying horse and the magic carpet.'

Igor Sikorsky

'The air is an extremely dangerous, jealous and exacting mistress. Once under the spell most lovers are faithful to the end, which is not always old age. Even those masters and princes of aerial fighting, the survivors of fifty mortal duels in the high air who have come scatheless through the War and all its perils, have returned again and again to their love and perished too often in some ordinary commonplace flight undertaken for pure amusement.'

Winston Churchill

Contents

CHAPTER ONE - A LESSON   6

CHAPTER TWO - STUDENT PILOT   14

CHAPTER THREE - ARMY SUPPORT   34

CHAPTER FOUR - SEARCH AND RESCUE   53

CHAPTER FIVE - BOND HELICOPTERS   79

CHAPTER SIX - OMAN   102

CHAPTER SEVEN - FIREFIGHTING   120

CHAPTER EIGHT - POLICE   125

CHAPTER NINE - YORKSHIRE AIR AMBULANCE   148

CHAPTER TEN - BACK TO THE FUTURE   167

EPILOGUE   182

Chapter 1

A Lesson

20 October 1984
D Flight 22 (Search and Rescue) Squadron
Leconfield, East Yorkshire

We've got a job!' Bob, the operations clerk, shouted to the crew room as he hit the 'Scramble' bell on the desk. A loud clanging started up in the hangar and people ran to their tasks preparing the helicopter. I jumped to my feet, rushed through to the ops room and started clambering into my immersion suit as Bob gave us rough details of the incident. The *Viscaria*—a Grimsby fishing boat with three men on board— had suffered engine failure 100 miles offshore and was under tow from another fishing boat. The weather was deteriorating quickly, with the vessel taking on water and threatening to go under.

A Lesson

When I say the weather was deteriorating, I mean it was bloody awful! A deep depression had just crossed England, giving gale force winds and howling rain. It had moved away eastwards, into the North Sea, just where our fishing vessels were struggling westwards, directly into the gale.

I grabbed my helmet and lifejacket, donning them as I went down the stairs which led to the helicopter pan. The Houchin external power supply was already connected and running as I clambered up the side of the big Wessex and removed the pitot cover just outside the cockpit side window. I swung my leg in, reaching for the straps of the backpack dinghy, which was my backrest, at the same time flicking on the battery switch and fuel pumps, then hitting the start button to get the first engine going. The cockpit had been prepared by me for a quick start at the beginning of the shift. I monitored the gauges jumping into life as I continued to strap in: first engine running, hydraulics and electrics good. I gave the signal to unplug the Houchin, checked the rotor brake pressure again, then set about getting the second engine going. When it was at a steady idle, I squeezed forward on the speed select to apply some torque before releasing the rotor brake and accelerating the engine to achieve full speed on the rotors. There was a switch to operate which got both engines driving the rotors, after pulling the port engine to idle. This took the engine from driving the accessories to driving the transmission and, when complete, the port engine was accelerated to match the starboard. Ready to go!

Up Gently

My crewmates had clambered on board after the rotors were running, acknowledging my 'thumbs up' before walking under the rotor disc. With me that day were winch operator Master Navigator 'Uncle' Ron Dedmen and winchman Master Air Loadmaster Eric Ainslie. Ron was the last non-commissioned navigator flying on front-line operations, having joined the RAF during WW2! There was not a more experienced winch operator on Search and Rescue. He joined me in the cockpit. Eric was also a very senior loadmaster, a wiry Geordie with a dry sense of humour. I couldn't have asked for a better crew.

A quick check that the winch was working correctly, then it was time to lift. Eric was checking for any other aircraft around, giving me 'Clear above and behind' as I squeezed up on the collective lever in my left hand, pushing the left pedal to counteract the torque swing to the right, then—as we broke ground—easing the nose forward to fly away. We cleared the shelter of our parking spot in the lee of the hangar and plunged into the gale force wind blowing from the west. Ron had given me an initial heading and I banked steeply to the left, levelling out on that track. The wind was behind us and, pulling full power, our airspeed was 110 knots, with a groundspeed closer to 160 knots! I checked in with Humberside Radar. 'No traffic'. Nobody else was daft enough to be airborne that morning.

En route we discussed our options. With the strong westerly wind, it was possible to continue on to Holland! The trouble was that I had no charts or frequencies for Dutch airspace. Plus, the bad weather was heading in that direction and could make life difficult. The other option was to land on one of the gas production rigs in the 'Rough' field and refuel before battling on towards Grimsby hospital landing site. Either option gave us about 20 minutes to winch up the survivors. The wind had now picked up and was blowing 70 knots, storm force 11, equal to hurricane strength one! I decided that we would refuel on the rig if all went to plan. Ron was navigating using the three Decca decoders in the cockpit and transposing the information onto a special map.

After about 35 minutes we spotted the stricken boat. I was surprised to see that the tow line was some 400 metres long but, of course, it made sense. The waves were now huge, I had never seen anything like it! From trough to crest was at least 40 feet and the howling wind was blowing spindrift from the crests, which occasionally were breaking, swamping the *Viscaria*. If she hadn't been under tow she would definitely have breached and gone under.

I came to a high hover alongside the boat so we could assess the winching options. Ron had flipped the cockpit seat up and disappeared down into the cabin. There was a small clear area on the stern where the three fishermen were huddled, hanging on as their vessel continued its roller coaster ride. That was our target area.

Eric prepared to be winched down into that hell. He was so concerned at the conditions that he opted to wear a backpack one-man dinghy; despite the hindrance it might be to his movement. It was the only time I knew a winchman to wear one.

The first thing to do was to lower a 'Hi-Line' to the deck. Basically, this was a weighted rope attached to the winch hook which would help the survivors guide Eric onto the deck next to them and allow a bit of leeway in the winching operation. It had instructions for them *not* to lash it to any part of the boat but to keep hold of it in their hands. It took a few attempts to get it to them, with the wind blowing so strongly it was trailing behind, even with the weights. Ron's steady monotone voice never changed in pitch as he directed me towards the target. I was concentrating harder than I had ever concentrated before. I had a knot in my stomach as I followed Ron's instructions and kept station with this bucking bronco of a trawler. Success! They had the Hi-Line!

Eric attached himself to the winch, Ron checked him over. Then he was out of the door, dangling on the wire and swinging in the wind. Again, we moved closer to the boat: Ron's voice as steady as a rock, me with a lump in my throat fighting to keep the big helicopter in the right position. I had sight of the front of the boat as we moved in, the masts were swinging wildly below me. The fishermen helped guide Eric towards them, Ron picked the perfect moment and placed Eric next to them. Relieved for a second, I moved back and left when told to, then watched as Eric prepared the first two survivors to be lifted, having taken two strops down with him. I glanced up and forward, which was a mistake, as all I could see was rank after rank of massive waves, stretching to the horizon! Ron directed us back to the overhead position and said 'up gently' when Eric gave him the thumbs up. Again, I moved back and left as Ron winched in the first two. When they got to the door Ron busied himself with seating them and strapping them in as I continued to look down on the *Viscaria*, now with just Eric and the skipper on board.

As I watched, she was pulled up another monstrous wave by the tow line. This time, as she approached the crest, the wave broke over the top of her, completely submerging Eric and the skipper. I thought she was finished but no! She appeared on the other side, surfing down into the trough. Eric looked up at me and, grinning, started banging his chest as if to restart his heart! I just thought 'mad bastard!' Ron was now ready, and we moved back for the final lift of Eric and the skipper. The manoeuvring seemed more difficult, or maybe I was tiring, but we got there and with another 'up gently' I moved up and away from the boat with a sense of profound relief. Ron had to deal with a swing on the wire as he winched up the other two blokes. Eventually they were at the door, then on board. 'Winching complete, door closed'. We had done it, and Eric hadn't needed to use his dinghy!

I set course for the rig, noting the much

slower groundspeed. It was only about 50 miles away, but it was going to take us an hour to get there. I closed my cockpit window and could smell the cigarette smoke drifting up from the cabin. Although it was not official policy, we carried an 'Emergency' packet in the first aid kit for survivors and it was always appreciated.

Landing on the rig helipad was fine, even with the gusting wind. At least it was stationary, and it was only us moving about! It was too windy to stop the rotors, so the deck crew gave us a 'hot' refuel. The galley staff had sent up some cakes and hot tea which were very welcome. Refuel complete, we prepared to leave for the Grimsby hospital landing site. I was about to learn a practical lesson on helicopter theory of flight.

As a helicopter starts to move forward from the hover and increase speed the 'clean' air entering the rotor disc from above helps the blades to turn and actually reduces the power needed to maintain height. However, moving increases the drag through the air, increasing the power required to maintain height. At a certain airspeed one cancels out the other and gives the minimum power needed to maintain height. This is the 'Minimum Drag Speed'. It is different for each helicopter and for the Wessex it was 65 knots. As I lifted from the pad, we were already doing 55-60 knots. I eased the nose forward, as I'd done hundreds of times before, expecting to fly up and away. But as soon as we started moving, I reached the minimum drag speed and the old bird needed a lot more power just to maintain height! We started sinking and my only option was to overtorque to 3,500 lbs, squeezing the nose further forward as I did so. We cleared the deck, but I reckon that the tail rotor missed it by inches. I had been flying the Wessex for six years now and had a good knowledge of how much fuselage was attached behind me. Had the tail rotor hit, we would have been spinning down into those waves or blown into the rig legs. But we made it! With hindsight and the wisdom of experience, I should have lifted vertically to at least 50 feet before moving forwards. Lesson learned.

As we continued towards the Grimsby hospital landing site the wind had dropped to force 7 or 8. The full welcoming committee was waiting: fire service, police, ambulance and coastguard. Word had got out and I believe some family members were there also. I kept the rotors running as Eric escorted the survivors out of the cabin and under the disc. He gave me a 'thumbs up' to return and I reciprocated. Job done, we lifted and returned to Leconfield where the blokes swarmed over the aircraft, getting it ready as soon as possible for any new missions coming in. Shift change was at lunchtime, so we were soon handing over to the incoming crew, who wanted all the details of what we had been up to! Then I cycled off home, still to be available if a second crew was required.

What had brought me to a job like this?

Chapter 2

Student Pilot

I always wanted to fly. No, I always wanted to be a pilot! When I was three years old my parents relocated from Glasgow to Newcastle-upon-Tyne and bought a house in a place called Wideopen (really!). From our lounge window I could watch the aircraft on the approach to Newcastle Airport. Piston airliners to begin with: Dakotas, Elizabethans, Constellations and the like. I was fascinated. Dad would take us to the airshow at RAF Acklington each year on Battle of Britain weekend where I was in heaven. At seven years old I flew as a passenger for the first time, from Newcastle to Basle and return, to spend the summer holidays with my aunt and uncle in Alsace. The aircraft was a BKS Airlines Airspeed Ambassador. Those were the glamour days of air travel and it cemented my desire to become a pilot. Everything I did in my school life after this was aimed at that ambition!

In 1973 I applied and was accepted for the BOAC/BEA training college at Hamble, on the Solent. All I had to do was pass my A level exams in the summer of '74, but I failed them! I had discovered club rugby, beer, cars and girls. My schoolwork slipped. Idiot!

Another year of study and, with exams passed, I re-applied, but they were not recruiting that year. What to do? I had not considered the military up to then but now, it was the obvious solution. I popped into the Royal Air Force recruitment centre in Newcastle, told them I wanted to be a pilot, then a world-weary Flight Lieutenant tried to talk me out of it! So many applied and so many were rejected, why not join the admin branch or engineering instead? I stuck to my guns and filled in the paperwork, then the Flt Lt had another chat with me, telling me that I had to pass the commissioning course before I would start flying. He described it as like a 'Four-month Scout camp', nothing to worry about. He was a bit economical with the truth!

Next was the Officer and Aircrew Selection Centre at RAF Biggin Hill. Interviews, exams, practical exercises and rudimentary coordination checks, very similar to the Hamble assessment. I was successful and my joining instructions to attend the Officer Cadet Training Unit at RAF Henlow arrived, to commence in July 1976.

My introduction to military life came as quite a shock. The constant inspections drove me to the point of wanting to jack it all in but friends on the same course, in the same predicament, talked me into continuing. I came to realise that the system was aimed at making you feel that way and seeing how you coped! We all helped each other through. A big character, in all senses of the word, was a friend on the course called

Dick Marshall. In our course photograph he was centre, in the back row, head above everyone else! He went on to train as a Navigator and was killed in a Canberra crash in Malta a couple of years later.

JETS

Four months later and I was now Acting Pilot Officer Sutherland, itching to go flying. My newly commissioned friends and I were posted to Number One Flying Training School at RAF Linton-on-Ouse in Yorkshire. On arrival we were issued with our flying gear and helmets and commenced ground school. We were going straight onto jets, the Jet Provost T3A, as the RAF operated an 'All Jet' syllabus at that time. Ground school was intense, just as much as the flying was to be intense. The 'Chop' rate was high and not much leeway was given for slow learners!

John Sutherland as an officer cadet (rear, middle).

Student Pilot

I was allowed some Christmas leave, but I knew my first flight was to be in the first week of January, when I returned. I can remember sitting in the kitchen in my parents' house going over and over the pre-start and other checks, which we had to know by heart.

Back at Linton and the big day arrived, 4th of January 1977. The weather was awful! Lots of cloud right up to 25,000 feet. Some gaps between layers, good Yorkshire weather. Good enough! A familiarisation flight to start with before the steep learning curve began. My checks were all good and my instructor demonstrated the take-off before we plunged into the cloud. He found us a gap and I was able to practise some basic handling between the cloud layers and get used to talking on the radio. He then locked on to the Instrument Landing System and before I knew it, the runway was there, and we were landing! I had been so busy with my checks and keeping up with what was going on that it was over in a trice.

Up Gently

The author (nearest) is commissioned.

After that first flight I was teamed up with my regular instructor, Flt Lt Al Riley. I was lucky in that I was playing rugby for the station team and Al and I were the two second-row forwards! The interaction between instructor and student was supposed to be very much on a 'Yes Sir, no Sir' basis but it was obviously more relaxed with Al. He was an ex-Vulcan pilot and always insisted that his students had to perform better than him! The two of us squeezing into a Jet Provost meant that the centre of gravity was way forward, so the trim wheel was always way back. I think it would surprise today's RAF students just how much drinking was done back then. Flying suits were allowed in the mess bar up to seven o'clock and it was normal to finish work and for students and instructors to 'Stack' to the bar at five!

Student Pilot

John Sutherland in the cockpit of a Jet Provost.

Disaster was to strike for me though. Airsickness. I was having problems on just about every flight. Al was very sympathetic, and we tried to work through it but it was no good. It was impeding my ability to keep up with the course and so I was grounded pending a referral to the RAF Aviation Medical branch. With great sympathy and understanding my mate on the course, Stuart Nuttall, gave me the nickname 'Bill' (said with a retching movement—lovely) and that name stuck with me through to my first squadron!

In the meantime, the station dentist, who was in charge of the rugby team, pulled some strings and got me a place with the RAF XV on their Easter tour of Cornwall. It was the highest level I had ever played at, and I was tight-head prop for the game against Penryn, who were English club champions at that time. On our team were

Up Gently

Scotland and British Lions legend Billy Steele and future England captain, John Orwin. We won three-nil, and it was bloody hard work!

Then off to RAF Farnborough and the Air Medical branch. Multiple tests were done on me before I commenced a two-week course on the 'Spin Table', a medieval torture chamber which was basically a chair in a box which rotated. The medical paper relating to it says 'The rationale of the treatment regime devised is based on the principle of relieving the patient's state of anxiety while building up his level of acclimatization to vestibular stimuli by means of repeated head movements on a rotating platform. These movements produce a cross-coupled or Coriolis stimulation of the semicircular canals resulting in a sensation which is frequently bizarre and confusing and leads to the onset of motion sickness if the stimulus is sufficiently severe and prolonged.' I also decided to pack in drinking until I could be sure that I would graduate! The spin table gradually decreased my susceptibility to motion sickness.

Following on from that I was sent to RAF Cranwell to fly with a doctor who was also a Qualified Flying Instructor (QFI). His name was Wing Commander Sean Marshall and, if it were not for him, you would not be reading this now. A fantastic, enthusiastic and inspirational figure, he got me through. He only flew the Jet Provost T5, a faster, more powerful version which had a pressurised cockpit. Starting off gently, we worked our way up to stalling, spinning and aerobatics. Then, possibly the worst manoeuvre for inducing sickness, the max-rate turn. From flying fast and level you rolled to 90 degrees of bank and, bang, pulled hard on the stick to 6g. Grunting to keep the blood from draining to your legs you would be looking through the cockpit roof to see where you were going, adjusting your height with bank. The speed would drain off with drag until you were pulling a steady 4.5g at 180 knots. Grunting and swivelling your head!

Wg Cdr Marshall decided that I had reached a standard where I could return to training. But first, he wanted me to go solo while on the Medical Rehabilitation course, something not done before! He arranged for me to do a check ride with an examiner from the Central Flying School, the unit he was attached to. So, on the 5th of July 1977 I flew to RAF Barkston Heath with Flt Lt Jonathan as my instructor, completed a few circuits and then he told me to taxi to the tower. We parked, opened the canopy and he got out saying, 'I've seen enough. Do one circuit, treat it like all the others, then return here to collect me'. I was on my own in a jet aircraft! I went through the checks meticulously as I taxied to the runway holding point. Cleared for take-off, I entered the runway. Final checks then wound the Rolls-Royce Viper up as I held it on the toe brakes, releasing them at 90% thrust, continuing to 100% and accelerating. Airborne! Touch the brakes and press the red 'Gear Up' button, a climbing left turn onto the downwind leg. It was only then I took a glance across the cockpit to see the empty seat and revel in the moment. Back to business, downwind checks, radio call 'Downwind to land', acknowledge the tower's 'Cleared to finals', calculate threshold speed, turn onto finals, recheck the undercarriage is down, 'Finals, three greens', full flap. Then I see the fire tenders and ambulance parked by the runway with their lights on! Standard practise for a student's first solo, I was to learn. I creamed it onto the runway, taxied round to the tower where my instructor was waiting, grinning. He climbed in and took the opportunity to get some flying, taking us back to Cranwell for a spirited 'run and break' before landing. I had flown my first solo! My new-found friends among the Cranwell cadets were very pleased for me, especially knowing the reason I had been sent there.

I returned to Linton-on-Ouse to the same training squadron but now on a later course, 21 course, with new course mates. I was allocated to a new main instructor, Flt Lt Dave Harle. I don't know what he thought of inheriting the 'sicky' student! He was a gentleman and eased me back gently into training. I was quickly sent solo back on the Mk3 and was flying as often as possible, rapidly increasing the intensity of manoeuvres, working up to aerobatics, spinning and max rate turns. Spinning was something which concentrated the mind. From straight and level, close the throttle and pull back on the stick until the aircraft stalled. Then kick full left rudder and continue pulling. The left wing would drop, the tail would yaw right and the nose would rise. You were now rotating around all three axes as you plummeted towards the ground! Hold everything for five turns, then operate anti-spin controls before pulling out of the dive. If the spin hadn't stopped by 8,000 feet you were to eject! Oh yes, Jet Provost flying was fun.

We were informed that there were slots available for two of us to move to helicopters after graduation. I jumped at the chance as I was still keen to gain a civilian licence, and this would be a way forward. I had a long chat with one of our instructors who had been a helicopter pilot, who gripped my interest, explaining how helicopter pilots had to be more flexible, able to think on their feet as the whole ethos of taking off and landing from almost anywhere demanded an ability to make quick (and correct!) decisions. I was hooked. Phil Roberts and I (Phil had the nickname 'Man Cub'. Think of Mowgli in the Disney cartoon ... it was Phil!) were selected for rotary. If we passed the Final Handling Test on jets.

The work-up towards that continued. We flew four Jet Provosts up to RAF Kinloss for a couple of weeks in order to continue the course, when the dreaded Vale of York fog set in. Back to Linton, where I planned and flew a land-away to RAF West Freugh with Dave Harle, including low-level, medium-level and high-level legs en route. We were 'bounced' at one point by another Jet Provost, which would normally be followed by a mini dogfight, trying to get on the other's tail. But we had our luggage in small panniers down the tail which restricted the maximum 'G' to 3, so we were easy prey and carried on our way, secure in the knowledge that we would have trounced him on any other day. On arrival at West Freugh the panniers prevented a hooligan run and break, but I made a sideslip final approach, full right rudder, full left aileron, straightening up at the last moment to place us gently on the runway. It looked good.

The new rugby season started, and I was selected for the trials match for the RAF XV. My flight commander, Flt Lt Dick Mott, was not happy. He told me that I could learn to fly, or I could play rugby and be back-coursed, possibly losing my slot on helicopters. It was an easy decision and the point where my illustrious rugby career crashed and burned! I carried on playing for station teams and was selected for a couple of Command level matches but no more top-level games.

My Final Handling Test was the day after my 22nd birthday, on the 22nd of December. I flew with Dave Harle in the morning, going over everything one last time, then after lunch into the test with Flt Lt Radley. I was ready and knew that my performance was good. Aerobatics went well, spinning was fine, then simulated engine failure along with a 'speechless' radio failure to return to Linton for a glide approach and landing. I can still remember High Key, 2,500ft abeam the threshold, turning downwind descending to Low Key 1,500ft downwind abeam the threshold before judging the final turn to land with the engine at idle. My landing was on the heavy side, as I remember! But good enough and I had passed.

Myself and the other blokes on the course arranged a celebration night out for ourselves and the instructors at the Wakefield Theatre Club. The Barron Knights were playing. We had bought a home brew kit for our Flight Commander, which was presented to him onstage. The compere took the mick remorselessly due to his name, Dick Mott! I shared a table that night with four others, two instructors, Dick and Al Riley and two other students, John Cathie and Steve Belcher. Within 5 years they were all to die in aircraft crashes.

HELICOPTERS

In the New Year of 1978, I was posted to Number 2 Flying Training School (Helicopters) at RAF Shawbury. There were six of us on the course. Four of us from Linton-on-Ouse: myself, Man Cub, Archie Cook and John Streeter, were joined by two 'Greenshielders' from RAF Cranwell, Dick Lacy and Dave Simpson. 'Greenshielder' was the affectionate term for those who joined with a university degree and were given accelerated promotion, their degree equivalent to Green Shield stamps of the time. Dick and Dave were great blokes, definitely of a different culture to the ruffians from Linton! John was a cockney geezer, a real Del-boy type and Archie was a Scotsman of style and flair. We were to fly the Westland Whirlwind Mk10 for basic training, changing up to the Wessex Mk5 for advanced training.

Ground school was first, of course, going

Up Gently

The author trained on the Westland Whirlwind.

over the technical side of the Whirlwind and introducing us to the principles of flight for a helicopter. That would be a book by itself (and they have been written!).

I have often been asked to explain how a helicopter flies. The answer can be very complicated but here is the basic Sutherland guide. To fly, you need power. For this the Whirlwind had a small jet engine in the nose, the Rolls-Royce Gnome. The exhaust from this drove a turbine wheel which, through driveshafts and gearboxes, turned the rotor head to which the main blades were attached. The force used to turn the rotors made the fuselage want to turn in the opposite direction. So a small rotor was put at the end of the tail, driven by a long shaft from the main rotor gearbox, pushing against that force to keep the whole shebang pointing the right way.

The rotors rotated at a set RPM. Their angle

could be altered to bite more or less as they rotated. Obviously, biting more means that they will try to slow down so more exhaust gas is needed to keep the turbine at the same speed, so more fuel is needed. For the Whirlwind, the fuel requirement was controlled by a very early computer which sensed the rotor rpm and adjusted the fuel input to keep it at the set rpm. As backup, there was a twist-grip throttle by your left hand to control the engine if the computer was to malfunction.

So, here you are, on the ground with everything turning. Imagine that spinning rotor as a disk. You have a lever in your left hand which you pull up to increase the bite of the blades all together. Collectively. It is called the Collective Lever. (No surprise!) The computer senses the blades slowing down with drag and inputs more fuel, adding power. More power to the main rotors makes the fuselage want to turn the other way so the tail rotor is made to 'bite' more by pushing the correct pedal at your feet.

You are lifting to the hover. In your right hand you hold a stick. It can vary the tilt of the disk in all directions by adding 'bite' at any point around the disk in a cyclic fashion. It is called the cyclic stick, and you can correct the drift with this—you get the drift? Anyway, when you tilt the disk, you move in the direction that you tilted it. This allows you to remain in one position or to move around. You push the pedals to increase or reduce the 'bite' of the tail rotor, making the fuselage rotate clockwise or anticlockwise.

And there you have it. All tail-rotor equipped

helicopters are basically the same. cyclic, collective, pedals and power. The power may be jet or piston and there may be one, two or even three engines. It is a little more complicated than that, of course. Each change in one of the four affects the other three, which all need monitoring and correcting! Ground school introduced us to all of this.

Next was principles of flight. Oh dear. They say there is brain surgery, rocket science and helicopter principles of flight! We were taught the wonderful world of induced flow, translational lift, inflow roll, tail rotor drift, etc, etc ...

The day came to put all this theory into practise. On 1 March 1978 I climbed up and into the Whirlwind cockpit and Charles 'Bill' Thompson climbed into the left-hand seat. Little did I know that for the next forty years I would be strapping myself into a few tons of rotating machinery! It was the only time I flew with Bill, after this first sortie we were allocated our primary instructors and mine was Tim Wood.

Flying the thing above 40 knots was straightforward, much like a fixed wing aircraft. It was below 40 knots when it became interesting in a hurry and the classroom description of the controls began to make sense. Our instructors began the process of eliminating our fixed-wing skills and (hopefully) instilling rotary-wing skills. Hovering was an obvious one and not something which came naturally. I needed a little extra time to get to grips with it, which is a bad description because my heavy-handed grip was the problem! I believe it was an older instructor, Mike Butt, who gave me the secret: 'Hold the cyclic like Lady Chatterley would hold the gamekeeper's dick. Fingertip pressure, not white knuckles.' It did the trick and was always at the back of my mind after that!

Hovering on the airfield was fine. What was more intimidating was returning to the pan to shut down. Manoeuvring between the parked helicopters and placing your steed back on its designated spot with your contemporaries watching from the crew room, ready to jeer or applaud as you walked through the door!

We would leave Shawbury and fly to the disused airfield at RAF Ternhill, or to a grass airfield at Chetwynd, to practise our circuits and hovering. Every trip with an instructor would also include at least one engine off landing following an autorotation. What is an autorotation? It is the helicopter equivalent of gliding, continuing to fly and maintain control without power to the rotors. They continue to turn due to a magic phenomenon known as 'Autorotative Airflow'. Think of the sycamore seed. As it drops, it rotates, which slows its descent and allows it to be blown by the wind. So, in the helicopter you are descending with the rotors turning and forward airspeed. You can manoeuvre to line up with a suitable landing spot. As you get close to that spot, you pull the nose up (flare) which does three things; it reduces your rate of descent, reduces your airspeed and increases the rotor speed, giving the rotors more energy for what is to follow! As the speed drops, you ease the nose forward and use the energy in the rotors for one almighty collective 'bite' which cushions your landing. The whole business is fraught with dangers. Flare too low and you could hit the ground hard and fast. Flare too high and your rotors could run out of energy before you can cushion the landing, so you will hit hard. Not dropping the nose means possibly hitting tail first. Dropping the nose too early means running onto the ground too fast. Pulling collective too late or too early will both give you a hard landing! I didn't envy the poor instructors who had to 'follow through' on the controls as their student tried to kill them both. We were given just one sortie for engine off landings solo. I'm sure it was dreaded just as much by the instructors as it was by us students. Three circuits into autorotation and engine off landing. That first time when you close the throttle and it all goes quiet, descending rapidly and you are totally committed, it concentrates the mind wonderfully! I understand that autorotations to a landing are not part of the curriculum any more. A shame.

We started to fly with a crewman in the cabin and crew cooperation became an important part of each trip. We were then introduced to underslung loads and the business of following instructions from the crewman. Towards the end of the course, we were attached to the Search And Rescue Flying School at RAF Valley on Anglesey for a couple of weeks which introduced us to winching and mountain flying. Winching on land was fine, 'Dry Winching', but learning the black art of winching over water was different altogether and not a practise mastered by every pilot. I was lucky in that I found the 'knack' for it pretty quickly. We then learned to winch people on and off a moving deck with a vessel from the RAF Marine Branch. My instructor for the deck trips was Flt Lt Dick Foster and he gave me a verbal kick in the arse which stuck with me through the rest of my flying. He called me out for a lack of dynamism dealing with my crew. It wasn't acceptable to just be the bloke who climbed in the front and went flying. The safety of all on board was in your hands and your interactions with your crewmates, as aircraft captain, had to assure them of your capabilities and leadership. Dick had dynamism in spades, of course, whereas I was still pretty maxed-out on flying the aircraft and I can't have been the life and soul when airborne! I resolved to make more of an effort after that debrief. The science of 'Crew Resource Management' had not even been thought of then but Dick was teaching it way before it evolved.

We returned to Shawbury and continued to train, working towards the final exercise scenario which involved everything we had learned. I had the pleasure of flying with our USAF pilot on an exchange tour, Capt. John Taylor, for most of that exercise. Then back to Shawbury and a final handling test with the boss, Sqn Ldr McGregor.

We now moved on to advanced training on

the Wessex. Two Gnome engines in the nose and a much bigger carrying capacity. The cockpit was not exactly ergonomic. A large flat Instrument panel festooned with circular dials and a small central warning panel. Other warning lights seemed to be placed randomly. We were given a couple of weeks of ground school to learn the technical side, then began the six-week flying course. 21st of August is a date I will always remember because it was the date of my second marriage in 2000, but also the day I first flew a Wessex in 1978! It felt enormous but powerful and safe. A very old design from the 1950s based on the Sikorsky S58T it was from pre-computer days when things were over-engineered for safety, it felt solid and dependable from the start.

We covered the same exercises done in the Whirlwind, low-level navigation, confined landing areas, underslung loads, night flying and Instrument flying, plus procedures for loss of one engine. My final handling test, which led to the allocation of my RAF wings, was on the 2nd of October. Our course were all presented with wings at a ceremony in the officers mess on the 6th of October. My parents were there and understandably proud. I had been posted to 72 Squadron (Army Support) flying the Wessex, which came up in conversation with a Wing Commander after the ceremony. My Dad was talking about a friend of his who had been in Bomber Command in World War 2, being shot at. The Wg Cdr said 'Oh, they'll be shooting at John soon enough when he gets to Northern

Student Pilot

Ireland!' I thought my mother was going to pass out and there was nothing the bloke could say to mollify her.

Chapter 3

Army Support

J ohn Streeter and Dave Simpson were posted to Sea Kings while me, Dick, Phil and Archie were to join our Squadrons at RAF Odiham. Dick and me to 72 Sqn and Phil and Archie to fly Pumas with 230 and 33 Sqns respectively.

Before we could be considered ready for tasking, we had to complete a couple of months with 240 Operational Conversion Unit. It introduced us to more advanced handling techniques and some ultra low-level flying for concealed approach and departures. We spent a good amount of time on instrument flying, leading to a first instrument rating. Everything else was covered, night flying, underslung loads, winching, formation flying and simulated tasks. The standards were high, and we were expected to reach them quickly.

Early in December 1978 I learned that Dick Marshall had died in a Canberra crash in Malta. He was riding on the rumble seat, while the crew of pilot and navigator both had ejection seats.

*The author was posted to 72 Sqn flying the
Westland Wessex.*

The aircraft suffered power loss on the take-off
run, due to fuel contamination, and was not able
to get airborne. The pilot and Navigator ejected,
leaving Dick inside as it careered off the end of
the runway and exploded into a fireball.

I don't know if that had any effect on me but
a couple of days later my first check ride didn't
go well, I'm afraid! I can't remember what the
problem was, but I failed it and was scheduled to
fly a couple of revision trips before a chop ride.
I will state here that I never considered myself
to be God's gift to aviation. I always had to work

hard to reach the required standard of the RAF, but I made sure that I did. Even if there were hiccoughs on the way!

My instructor for those revision trips was an amazing bloke called Taff Walker. He was a Master Pilot, one of the last non-commissioned pilots still flying who had flown in WW2. He always had a pipe in his mouth and his faithful Labrador was always with him. He recognised how stressed I was, and we went over everything again. When he was happy that I would pass, he put me forward for the check ride. There was no question, but I had to pass this, or I would not be joining my Squadron! I had the same examiner, Flt Lt Hugh Northey, an ex-Queens Flight pilot who I found intimidating, but Taff had prepared me well and Hugh was happy to pass me this time, as an operational Wessex pilot.

72 Squadron

January 1979 and I started earning my keep with the RAF. First, though, the Squadron training office checked me out. General handling, Instrument flying, navigation and night flying. Then I was immediately deployed to Salisbury Plain on exercise with the Army for a week. It was great to be actually doing a job, rather than training all the time. Back to Odiham for a short time before deploying to Stanford training area in East Anglia to live and work with Royal Marines 42 Commando in their work-up towards a Northern Ireland tour. Following that I was out to Northern Ireland for my first deployment. It was a pattern which continued for the rest of

Army Support

*On operations in Northern Ireland with Barry
Paton and Tim Bond.*

my time with 72. Exercises in UK and Germany,
tasking in UK, and regular deployments to
Northern Ireland on anti-terrorist operations. I
spent less time on base at Odiham than away!

My first detachment to Northern Ireland
came at the end of February. In Northern Ireland
we were based at RAF Aldergrove, across the
runway from the civil airport. Our squadron had
eight Wessex on permanent detachment, and we
shared the tasking with four Wessex from 845
Naval Air Squadron. The Officers' Mess was an
old building but we were housed in comfortable
portacabins.

A lot of alcohol was consumed. There was the
Mess Bar, of course, with Walter the barman, and
a 'Scruffs Bar' tucked away at the back, where

Up Gently

With colleagues in Northern Ireland in 1981.

beer was on tap with an honesty chit system 24 hours a day. Crews returning from tasks at various hours could go straight in and have a drink, or we could pile in there when the main bar closed! The old rule was 'eight hours, bottle to throttle' which had to be observed. Of course, this didn't guarantee sobriety after eight hours but it was playing the game! There was always one crew on standby for night callouts and they were not to drink, of course.

On my first night standby, I was crewed with my flight commander, a Squadron Leader who I shall leave nameless. The Squadron boss, Wing Commander Tony Ryle, was visiting Aldergrove at the time and I'd flown as his copilot on a task a couple of days earlier. We always flew with two pilots in the province due to the armed threat.

We also had a piece of armour plating which folded down on each cockpit side window to allow access. I digress. That evening I watched television in the ante room and stayed away from the bar. I popped in there later on to grab an orange juice. My flight commander was there, with the squadron boss, and it was obvious that they were putting the world to rights over a few beers! What should I do? Remind my flight commander that he was on standby and embarrass him in front of the boss? Or keep quiet and hope there was no callout? Callouts were rare occurrences, so I opted for the latter and disappeared quietly to bed, followed by sod's law!

Awakened from my sleep by the mess steward, I was told that there was a task. I threw my flying suit on and legged it to the hangar where Sgt 'Tolly' Tolhurst was already there, and the flight commander appeared a few minutes later. We were tasked to fly to Lisburn, pick up a bomb disposal bloke plus his 'Wheelbarrow' remote unit and deliver him to Magherafelt for a job there. The Sqn Ldr told me to fly, he would be my copilot. Not much choice really, as you could smell the alcohol as he spoke! It was a pitch-black night, with big snowstorms rolling through from the west. The trip down to Lisburn was fine and routing around Lough Neagh to Magherafelt went OK. The previous April a Scout helicopter had crashed into the lough after flying into a snowstorm. As we lifted to return to Aldergrove the snow was starting to fall. We were routing east, initially, away from the weather before turning south. As we did so the snow started again, and the airport lights were dimming. We just made it to a landing outside the hangar before we were engulfed in a blizzard! Five minutes later and it would have been very uncomfortable for this new pilot on his first Northern Ireland deployment. My flight commander was very sheepish, and we never spoke about what he had done. But it was always there.

In May, two helicopters were to deploy to West Germany for a big NATO exercise. I was lucky enough to be selected, we went in formation, crossing the Channel and routing to RAF Gutersloh to join 18 Sqn (another Wessex Sqn). I was crewed up with Flt Sgt John Shackleford for the duration and he took this new young pilot under his wing, teaching me the ins and outs of living comfortably on exercise. We were attached to one of the 18 Sqn flights as the exercise began, deploying out to live in the country for a couple of weeks and I really enjoyed myself. Daily tasks pouring in, mock attacks on our field locations requiring 'Crashouts' meaning starting immediately and moving to a pre-briefed new campsite. On one task we completed a battalion attack requiring 20 Wessex. Guess who was flying as number 20?

Landing with a full load on board as 19 other Wessex touched down in the same location was a new experience and with the air recirculating all around, plus my desire not to be late to the party, I made a pretty firm landing with my collective under my armpit! 18 Sqn boss, the fearsome Wing Commander Sandy Hunter, was on the ground at the drop site and I could see him clapping his hands, smiling, and running up and down. I think he was pleased.

One day John and I were tasked to fly ten journalists up to the 'Front Line' to visit the US 2nd Armored Division, 'Hell on Wheels'. I was issued with the correct IFF codes (Identification Friend or Foe) to fly so far forward. I gave the journos a spirited low-level ride all the way, then it was interesting as we came in to land, I could see the barrels of their anti-aircraft equipment following me! We shut down and handed over our passengers. Meanwhile, a young Lieutenant, about my age, escorted us to their field kitchen for lunch. What an eye-opener! Our American friends certainly ate well on exercise. John had schooled me that every time we were on task, we should take advantage of any eating facilities we land near, even just some blokes brewing a cup of tea, never go past food. For ourselves we were mainly living on Compo rations, 24-hour ration packs which included the basics. So, we tucked in like Kings with the 2nd and must have looked like the cats that had the cream when our passengers reappeared for the return trip, which was a bit more sedate!

When the exercise finished, we returned to Odiham and I was immediately off out to Northern Ireland again. June came and it was time for my six-month check rides. All professional pilots, military or civilian, have their ability checked every six months. Imagine having your driving test, in the rush hour, in bad weather, and every six months? It was just part of being a pilot, but I was always like a bear with a sore head for the days leading up to it. I failed the night flying check. This was the last check ride I was to flunk, I made damn sure I was ready for those which followed, but this time, Sgt Tom Cuthell had expertly guided me in picking up a heavy underslung load and I flew off into a circuit. Then my examiner, Flt Lt Brian Mansfield, failed an engine on me downwind. Not a problem in a Wessex, unless an idiot pilot was to let the speed fall below 65 knots (remember chapter 1?) and didn't have the power to maintain height as the speed continued to reduce. I still feel foolish writing this now! It got to the point where, in real life, I would have jettisoned the load to gain speed and height, but Brian took control, reinstated the engine and we headed home. The debrief was short and sweet, then Brian and I headed off to the Scruffs Bar where a longer debrief took place until the early hours! I went back to Odiham, did a couple of trips with the training office then re-sat the check ride with Support Helicopters legend, Flt Lt Dick Langworthy. I was out to impress after screwing up and Dick was happy with what he saw. As I said, there would be no more cockups on tests for me!

Boxes ticked and back out to Northern Ireland. Busy, as always. There were always one or two Wessex deployed daily to South Armagh, bandit country on the border with the Republic. We were based at Bessbrook Mill for 24 hours at a time. We generally flew as low as possible to avoid small arms fire. The IRA had at least one heavy-calibre machine gun and there were always rumours of a SAM-7 heat seeking missile in the province. It was a large Army camp and a very busy heliport, with tasking controlled from 'Buzzard's' hut next to the helipads.

On 27 August I was due to fly down there along with Flt Lt Syd Exton and Sgt John Mellor. We were in the ops room in the afternoon, preparing for our shift when we heard that there had been a couple of large explosions on the main road at Warrenpoint. The colleagues we were due to replace had been caught in the second explosion but limped back to Bessbrook in their damaged Wessex with injured survivors from the first explosion on board. We had to get airborne straight away and head to the incident location for casevac. Heading south, I called the unit on scene with our ETA and could hear gunfire on the radio reply. It was mainly Parachute Regiment soldiers who had been blown up and the survivors were shooting at anything that moved! The IRA had placed the first bomb in a trailer loaded with hay bales in a lay-by. They had put a second bomb next to a large stone wall, guessing that survivors of the first would muster there. They had guessed right and, when the first Wessex arrived, they detonated the second bomb. We were next to land, on the road. It was a scene of utter carnage, something I will never forget, bodies and bits of bodies everywhere. Paras came running up to us carrying badly wounded soldiers and John, in the cabin, piled in as many as possible for the five-minute flight to Bessbrook. Once there, we collected some troops and body bags before heading back to the scene.

The rest of the day was spent shuttling back and forth with injured and then the deceased in body bags, supported by an 845 Sqn Wessex which had followed us down. In the evening we had a few minutes break for a cup of tea at Buzzard's hut. I remember asking John Mellor a question and he delved into his flying suit calf pocket for a notebook. He pulled it out covered in blood, in fact both of his legs were soaked up to the knees. The cabin in our Wessex was not a pretty sight and we spent some time swabbing it out. As darkness fell, we took a couple of the worst injured to Musgrave hospital for treatment, returning to Bessbrook for a few hours kip before completing the next day's tasking. It had been the worst day in the province for the British Army. Sixteen members of the Parachute Regiment died, six from the first explosion and ten in the second, along with the commanding officer of the Queen's Own Highlanders and his signaller. It was also the day on which the IRA assassinated Lord Mountbatten, two children and one other adult in an explosion on his boat. A grim day.

The Officers Mess at Odiham was short of space and so some of us junior officers were moved out to share houses in the married quarters. Myself, Dick and another were in one house. The other housed Archie, Man Cub and a mate on 72, Andy Pulford. Their domicile was named 'The Swamp' for some reason but both houses were great places for entertaining and letting our hair down away from the mess! Andy had gone through Henlow ahead of us and had also joined 72 just before Dick and me. A good friend and a great help when joining the squadron, as he had been through it just before us. I even let him have a thrash on my old Triton motorbike after I had rebuilt it following an engine seizure. (That's another story, but not for here). Little did we know that Andy was to have a stellar career culminating in him being the first helicopter pilot to be Chief of the Air Staff!

I was lucky enough to have leave for Christmas and New Year, heading to my parents' house for some R&R. Two days after Christmas I saw the terrible news on the BBC that an RAF Puma helicopter had crashed in Zimbabwe. It turned out to be Archie Cook and a 'Greenshielder' friend Mike Smith, along with the crewman, Bob Hodges. They had been flying too low, suicidally low, following a road when they encountered some wires crossing the road. The wires hit the rotor head, control was lost, and they smashed into the ground, exploding into a fireball. No survivors.

Back to Odiham to begin 1980 with a month of tasks in the UK and my dreaded check rides. Which were all passed, as they would be for the rest of my career! The first half of this year followed the usual pattern of tasking on the mainland and long detachments to Northern Ireland. In March a new pilot joined our Flight, Flying Officer Scott Weir. He'd come through training a couple of courses behind me. A large, brash, confident and athletic Glaswegian, he was definitely someone you'd want on your side in a fight! A gifted sportsman, he scored 102 not out for Scotland against the MCC at Lord's. I didn't like him. Too bloody cocksure and loud, needed to get some time in. I told him so in the crew room one day and he threw a punch. Now, I reckoned to be able to handle myself, I'd been playing top-class rugby, but I was no match for Scott. The ensuing fight, (more like a bundle), saw him definitely get the better of me and I thought he would break my windpipe in a headlock! After that we had a mutual respect and in fact became good mates. For the rest of my time on the Squadron I was always in and out of trouble along with him, but we certainly enjoyed ourselves.

1980 was not a good year for three of the four table mates from Wakefield Theatre Club. On 28 May John Cathie was flying his Jaguar in a formation, returning to RAF Bruggen, when he inexplicably broke too early and smashed into one of the other aircraft. He died instantly and the other pilot ejected safely. On the 11th of July Dick Mott was flying a Phantom in close trail to another, being filmed for a BBC documentary. He was required to do a 'Canadian Break', a 270°

roll and fly away. He let the nose drop on the roll and crashed to the ground, exploding into a fireball. On 17 November Steve Belcher was co-pilot in a Nimrod taking off from RAF Kinloss. The aircraft hit a flock of birds, sustaining serious damage, crashing into a forest. The crew escaped the wreckage but Steve and his captain, an Australian pilot on exchange, were killed. I was starting to realise that this flying business could be risky!

Looking back, a few highlights of the year stick out. I was attached to the flight Andy Pulford was on and flew a couple of Northern Ireland tasks with him on the 4th and 5th of June. Who'd have guessed where he was headed? Not me, he seemed far too nice a bloke to be a senior officer, let alone in charge of the whole bloody outfit! September saw Exercise 'Crusader' in West Germany and this time the whole flight was deployed to the field there. Then in November, back in Northern Ireland, I reached a total of 1,000 hours flown. I was on a training trip for Instrument flying, wearing a 'hood' which restricted my vision to the panel. Flt Lt Roy Citrine was the safety pilot, and he gave me a talk down. When I reached the decision height, I removed the hood, and we were over Giants Causeway! We landed there and Roy shook my hand for completing my 1,000 hours. We headed back to Aldergrove and Roy bought me a celebration pint or two that evening! He was to die in a crash thirty months later. Christmas was spent in South Armagh doing a day's tasking for the army. The IRA weren't taking a holiday!

January 1981 saw me back at Odiham for a few tasks but also my check rides again! Day handling, night flying, instrument flying, and tactical support flying. Remarkably, February and early March saw me remaining at Odiham for Army tasks around southern UK, before heading back to Northern Ireland in late March for an eight-week detachment. We had a new Flight Commander, Sqn Ldr Derek Nequest, and he was a breath of fresh air compared with my night standby boss. Derek had inherited a motley, professional crew, who knew what they were doing and how to do it. Then how to celebrate! He was one of the lads when we were letting our hair down, but a respected boss.

The Squadron relocated the mainland base to RAF Benson, ahead of a permanent move out to Aldergrove. Scott and I had a final party in our married quarter at Odiham, having been warned that the Wing Commander was going to inspect it before we moved out. After the party we piled on to a Hercules out to Aldergrove, thinking that we had a few weeks before the inspection but, no! He came to inspect that morning, with bodies and booze still lying around, like the Wreck of the Hesperus! When we landed, Scott and I were met by the Senior Pilot, marched into the Detachment Commander's office and told to get back on the Herc and report to the Wing Commander at Odiham the next day, in best uniform! Which we did, receiving a bollocking for which I'd have to give 10 out of 10. We were given two days to get the house straight, then he was returning to inspect the house, and us, on Sunday morning. This was Friday and it turned out that a Squadron mate, Pete Quick, was having a party at his house in Basingstoke that night. So we went! Drummed up support there, so on Saturday we had an army of volunteers to help clean the house. Sunday morning arrived and Scott and I were stood to attention outside the house. The Wg Cdr arrived in civvies along with one of his children, gave the place a thorough once-over and gave us both a black mark on our records. I could sense some amusement as he did it, or I could have been wrong?

June and July were spent flying out of Benson on tasks to support and train land forces. On one task to Salisbury Plain, myself and my crewman Sgt Graham Andrews took along a WRAF officer for the day. We were training some Army lads in preparing and hooking up underslung loads. We had a busy day's flying and I think the blokes enjoyed the female company. Two things were of note that day; I reached 1,000 hours total Wessex flying, and as we left, with our WRAF in the co-pilot's seat, we did our usual departure beat-up, to be met with all the blokes, trousers down, bent over and mooning us!

August was a busy month in Northern Ireland, as the terrorist hunger strikers died one by one, we would attend the funerals in the province with a Wessex full of troops just in case trouble kicked off. Late in the month Scott and I had a task to the Bridge of Orchy Hotel in Scotland to collect crates of special 72 Sqn whisky bottled by the hotel, where we had a close relationship. We arrived at lunchtime and tossed a coin to see who would fly back and who would sample the wares. I lost and had to fly. We should have been two pilots up front to return to Aldergrove but we both recognised that he would be more comfortable in the cabin. Which was fine until he decided to open the cabin door, climb up the side of the fuselage and open my window/door to grab the cyclic and try to kill us! He was persuaded to get back inside by my right elbow before he did so! I wish I had kept one of those bottles, but they were demolished one night in the mess bar.

A couple of days later myself, Scott and Sgt Tim Storrs were given a briefing by an Army Intelligence officer for a task to collect troops near Strabane and insert them tactically to make an arrest. It was classified 'Top Secret' and we were handed a map with that logo printed in every corner! After take-off we were flying at about 2,000 feet when Scott decided to open his window. The map flew out. I cranked us over to the right, Tim spotted the map first, fluttering down towards farmland. I kept it in sight and landed close to it in a farmer's field. Tim got out, rifle slung over his shoulder, to collect the map. Scott and I decided to prank him, and I took off to disappear over the horizon. Poor Tim, stood in a field in Northern Ireland, carrying a rifle and holding a top-secret map! I feel awful about it as I write this now, but at the time, Scott and I were laughing like drains. We went back to collect him and the map, he was livid. He only spoke the bare minimum for the rest of the trip, staying professional but obviously cheesed off. I don't blame him!

After some September leave I returned to Aldergrove for my last stint. The Squadron was to move out to Aldergrove permanently on 12 November and that is the date that I was moving on. On 5ᵗ November I was operating out of Bessbrook, co-pilot to Fg Off Steve Petherick. We were moving underslung loads of building material down to Crossmaglen base. It must have been the fourth load when Sgt Thomas, directing Steve, said, 'Over the load, up gently, load off the ground, load clear of the fence'. Steve replying, 'Roger transitioning'. Then, from the crewman 'Load gone! Load gone!' As the Wessex leapt skywards a ton of building material slammed into the ground just feet from where a bloke was out walking his dog! We checked our load release buttons which were all safe and closed. The subsequent investigation revealed that it was a faulty net, one of the hooks had detached allowing the load to fall out. But missing the lucky dog-walker.

Towards the end of my time on 72 I took the exams required to gain my civilian pilot's licence. A kind soul had left a file in the training office detailing the steps to be taken. As Bristow Helicopters were still flying civilian-registered Wessex, I was able to take my flight test in one of our squadron's aircraft. (Thanks Syd Exton!)

My last Day in Ireland was picture-perfect

weather. I was to fly with Lt Norman Lees, our tame Royal Navy exchange pilot, two crewmen, Flt Sgt Jennings and Sgt Hamilton, and we were to head off to Enniskillen for a day's tasking around the beautiful lakes there. I couldn't have wished for a better final day. In the afternoon the rest of the Squadron's helicopters arrived from Benson and there was a ceremony to formally welcome the Squadron to the Station. A few beers were drunk that night. Norman was to die in a crash in 2000.

Chapter 4

Search and Rescue

My posting arrived and I was to join 22 Sqn D Flight at Leconfield, East Yorkshire, flying the Wessex on single-pilot day/night/IFR SAR duties. I first had to attend the Search And Rescue Training Unit at RAF Valley for three weeks in December to brush-up my winching and receive more detailed instruction on mountain flying. Final check was on 22 December so I had a Christmas trip to visit my parents before pitching up at Leconfield, the first week in January 1982.

22 Squadron
Leconfield, in East Yorkshire, had been an RAF station but had been handed over to the Army School of Mechanical Transport and renamed 'Normandy Barracks'. The runway and taxiways had been changed to represent roads and dual carriageways with road signs and

traffic lights and there was a constant stream of Bedford lorries and Land Rovers. D Flt occupied one hangar on the southeast corner of the pan. We had two Wessex which were custard-coloured, of course, a change from the cabbage-coloured army support version. It was a small unit, four pilots, four navigators/winch operators, and four crewmen. The engineers were all volunteers for the job and were all Corporal rank or above, due to the front-line, high priority assigned to SAR.

My first couple of days were spent being checked out by the SAR Wing QHI/Examiner, Flt Lt Tommy Taylor, a Geordie with a magnificent handlebar moustache, and a reputation for not tolerating fools! He didn't see me as one of those and was happy to put me on shift. For myself, I was really pleased to be putting my skills to good use, with the prospect of possibly saving lives in the future. The blokes on the flight made me feel at home straightaway even though I must have been the youngest pilot on the Squadron at that time. The groundcrew were all highly professional and I was to make good friends among the lads who were closer to my age. Over time we were all using first names. The rank structure was still there if there were visitors but otherwise it was a small professional outfit that did a job without the need for 'Yes Sir! No Sir!'

We worked 24-hour shifts, changing at midday, with bedrooms on site. Once off shift we were still available to be called in if a second crew was required. On shift we would plan a

Search and Rescue

Search and Rescue flying at Leconfield.

training sortie for the afternoon, or night flying if needed, then a training trip the next morning. Every six months the RAF Marine Branch would be based close by, and we would practise our deck winching with them. At other times the local fishing boats were extremely helpful, allowing us to practice winching on and off their decks. We would carry that day's newspaper and a fresh pint of milk to give them and sometimes they would give the winchman a basket of fish. They were always glad to see us!

My first Rescue wasn't until 10 April. There had been a couple of false alarms in the previous months, but this was the real thing. Two girls had been cut off by the rising tide under the cliffs south of Whitby. A very straightforward lift for Sgt Steve Lynch on the winch controlled by Uncle Ron. But it was a start!

Meanwhile, on the 2nd of April, Argentina had invaded the Falkland Islands. It was not to affect me directly, but the Sea Kings of 202 Sqn were earmarked for SAR duties in the South Atlantic. This meant that we would be providing one Wessex and a crew on detachment to RAF Coltishall, North of Norwich, for the near future. I note in my logbook a flurry of activity from 5 to 8 May, travelling up to the Rescue Coordination Centre at Pitreavie for a briefing, on to the Wessex flight at RAF Leuchars, then down to Coltishall to discuss the handover. Then back to Leconfield before going to SAR Wing headquarters at RAF Finningley on the 14th to receive a briefing from the Wing Commander Ivan Hughes, and the Squadron boss, Sqn Ldr Hammond-Doutre.

In late June we were involved as an aid to the police in North Yorkshire, searching for Barry Prudom, a gunman and serial killer who had had SAS training. Eventually he took his own life when discovered. It was my first taste of police flying!

On the 8th of July we were scrambled to search for survivors from a Phantom which had crashed in the North Sea. It was one of three which had departed RAF Valley earlier, one went straight to their home base of RAF Coningsby, while the other two flew practice intercepts at low level. The sea was flat calm, almost glassy, very unusual for the North Sea. The weather was hazy, no horizon and banks of low cloud. We searched for a good while but found no wreckage, just a large slick of oil and fuel. The Navy subsequently managed to recover about one third of the wreckage. When we got back to base, I discovered the name of the pilot. Al Riley, my Jet Provost instructor and rugby second-row mate. It was difficult staying focused for the rest of the shift.

July '82 was the time of the first Middle Wallop Heli-Meet, hosted by the Army Air Corps. An international helicopter competition and display. I must have pleased the boss, Robin Hammond-Doutre, as he selected me as the Squadron representative, with my crew, Flt Lt Andy Millar as navigator and Flt Sgt Warwick Laken, winchman. The competition had many facets including winching, navigation, timed circuits, search for survivor, combat vehicle recognition and flour bombing! We were

Winners of both the concours d'élégance and sword for overall runners up, at the first Middle Wallop Heli-Meet in July 1982.

crewed together for the whole month to practise together. The biggest challenge was the flour bombing. It had to be from 500 feet to a target on a disused runway. Eventually Warwick made a rudimentary bombsite from bits of old wood, and it did the trick. We could be pretty accurate. The boss was determined that we should do well, but the most important thing was to finish higher than the Sea King from 202 Sqn! Our Squadron standards officers, Flt Lt Steve Garrod (pilot) and Master Air Loadmaster Bob Pountney (winchman), spent two days with us going over every aspect of the competition. For the next two weeks we practised on every shift.

Monday 19 July was the day we took the spare Wessex and flew down to Middle Wallop, stopping at RAF Finningley en route to pick up the boss. When we arrived at Wallop, engineers leapt on board to disable any radio navigation equipment. It all had to be map and compass on the competition. There was an afternoon briefing for all crews, then we were bussed out to hotels in the local area. Back to the airfield the next morning at our allotted time, the blokes had her all ready. We launched off to begin our tasks under scrutiny. The winching competition was done in the grounds of Highgrove House, Prince Charles' residence, and it comprised lifting a bucket of water, taking it through a slalom course at a set height, then depositing it upright onto a target, spilling as little as possible! Oh, the high-tech world of helicopters. In 'Search for Survivor' we were given an area of map to look for a supposed downed pilot who would mark his position with a parachute. Andy had the inspired thought to look at the Ordnance Survey map and find wooded areas with clearings, then search those first. Bingo! The first one we went to had a parachute laid out and some bloke waving at us. Or was it two fingers? We were reasonably happy with the rest of the competition, our flour bomb hit the target. The results were to be announced at a dinner on Thursday night.

As soon as we landed, our engineers were on to the aircraft. There was a Concours d'élégance competition, being judged on Thursday. The engineering Flight Sergeant from Leconfield, John Lovelace, was determined to win it. He was a hard taskmaster to the blokes, cleaning and polishing everything, even inside the exhaust pipes! Our old Wessex was gleaming.

The Army had laid on entertainment for all those attending the competition. There was a stage erected in one of the hangars and each day there were bands, comedians, go-go dancers and strippers. Today's woke brigade would have had a fit, but we all enjoyed ourselves immensely and a lot of beer was drunk, especially back in the hotel.

Thursday evening's dinner was black tie and held in a suitably posh hotel. Crews and judges were from all over the world with the trophies being handed over by Air Chief Marshal Sir David Craig, who was Chief of the Air Staff (CAS): the boss of the RAF. Pulford's future job! When the meal was finished and before the speeches and presentations, bottles of Black Label Scotch were distributed liberally among the tables, courtesy of Boeing Helicopters. They were greatly appreciated. We were the overall runners-up! And won the Concours d'élégance. The winners were from the Central Flying School, Sqn Ldr Mike Chappel and his crewman MALM John Donnelly. Myself and Mike were each presented with a whacking great Wilkinson Sword, John Lovelace received a silver cup and 202 Sqn had the consolation of winning the winching section of the competition. Although winning a trophy, I was still a bit upset that we hadn't come first. One of the judges, a Jamaican Wing Commander who was on our table, let me know that we had lost by just four points in two thousand, a close call, which made me feel better. Robin Hammond-Doutre was grinning from ear to ear! I think the boss was pleased. Later, as we were leaving, John Donelly and I had a drunken mock swordfight. I'm surprised that nobody was killed!

Friday, Saturday and Sunday saw the airfield open to the public with all of the helicopters on static display. There was also a big flying display each day culminating in the Red Arrows. We had VVIP visitors on Friday: the Duke of Edinburgh and King Hussein of Jordan, with his son Prince Abdullah. The Duke had arrived in a Queen's Flight Wessex and was most impressed with the condition of ours. One of the lads told him that they could spruce up his helicopter, if he wanted! Cue a black look from John Lovelace.

Search and Rescue

The display days were fantastic, the weather stayed fair. It was interesting wandering around the aircraft park. At one point there was a pre-WW1 aircraft, a Sopwith Tabloid. I got chatting to the pilot, who was about to display, and had a peek inside the cockpit. Of its era, it had bugger all on the panel apart from a couple of rudimentary dials, but also a small modern sticker had been placed there which said, 'Aeroplanes bite fools!' A wise thought. I held the tail for this gentleman as he started, releasing him when he waved.

We departed for Leconfield on the Monday, dropping the boss off at Finningley on the way. He was a happy bloke but still wanted a full written report from me on the whole competition experience. The local press were out in force when we arrived back, we were very pleased with ourselves!

We then settled in back at work, shifts at Leconfield and at Coltishall. Lots of training trips interspersed with the odd scramble, nothing out of the ordinary. Lifted four people from a yacht stuck in the mud of the Humber estuary in late September. It was strange having the thing completely stationary and not trying to wrap the winch wire around its mast.

I was at Coltishall in November and an unusual task was passed to us. The Royal Navy had been persuaded to trial an autogyro for deck landings and we were to act as 'Plane Guard' in the event of any problems. The man who had done the persuading was Wg Cdr Ken Wallis, the ex-RAF pilot and brilliant inventor who had perfected the design of the autogyro. In the James Bond film, *You Only Live Twice,* he was the stunt pilot flying his own *Little Nellie* in an aerial dogfight sequence. He turned up at our unit a few days before the task, along with the Navy representative, for a briefing.

I'll quickly give the Sutherland take on autogyros: They are in permanent autorotation which keeps the rotor spinning (remember the sycamore seed?). A helicopter disk needs power to turn the disc and suck the air in from above, whereas an autogyro disc needs forward movement from a propeller to push the air up from below, which turns the disc and 'bite' can be added to produce lift. An autogyro cannot hover. It can land at very low, almost zero speed, but it needs forward movement to produce lift.

10 November and our Navy vessel, HMS *Leeds Castle*, with large helideck, was in position off Great Yarmouth. We positioned ourselves on the port side, ready for the worst and so that the Navy photographer, who we had on board, could record the event. The landing was not a problem, with five knots of headway on the ship, Wg Cdr Wallis was able to touch down with zero relative speed. The take-off was a different story! The autogyro was positioned on the back right corner of the deck, the ship turned 30° right to give a wind over the deck. With the propeller running a clutch was engaged to start the rotors spinning and the Wg Cdr set off. Just when I thought he might hit the superstructure in front, he lifted off, rolled left and dived towards the sea. I was

sure he would ditch but, just in time, the little machine dragged its wheels up from the waves and he flew away. The Navy had seen enough, and he was refused a further approach! We escorted him back to his base and headed home.

It was at this time that I had decided to branch out, away from the RAF. It may seem crazy, but I was having a great time, enjoying the flying and the atmosphere on the unit. But I knew that this tour would come to an end and the chances are that I could get a ground posting. Even moving to a flying slot on a large station didn't appeal, so I submitted my request for Premature Voluntary Retirement (PVR), knowing that it would be at least two years before I would be released as I still had ten years to serve. I had bought my first house in the nearby town of Beverley, a beautiful English Market town with a magnificent minster, and I was making friends in the local community. The real RAF seemed a million miles away. The boss, Robin, came to visit me at Leconfield hoping to change my mind. I told him that if I was guaranteed ten years at Leconfield then I would sign up straightaway, but of course that was not happening. He saw a career for me, but I wanted to make my own way in the flying world. My PVR was approved, I would be discharged on 1 December 1984.

1983 would be a year to remember! It started routinely, lots of training trips. We were constantly practising and honing our skills. One of our navigators was Graham Clark, an excellent winch operator and winchman. But Graham spoke with an occasional stammer! Never when flying or talking the pilot into position, only when away from the helicopter. If it had ever happened through training, or on the Squadron, he would have been grounded but he was as solid as a rock on the job.

For all the training we did, we never trained for winching at night. We were available 24 hours a day, of course, but night winching was just done as required. Lifting a survivor from the sea would have been a very difficult task with very few references to maintain a hover. Only one landing lamp, no night vision goggles then! Winching from a moving vessel obviously provided more references for the pilot but could still be extremely tricky depending on the size of the vessel and the sea state. Cliff winching had its own difficulties but at least it was stationary! I must admit that I was concerned about what my first night job would be. It wasn't to happen until I had been on the Squadron for over a year.

I was at Coltishall with Graham Clark and Flt Sgt Steve Lynch, a dour Yorkshireman who had a passion for his job who was as professional as you can get. The call came about midnight, a drug overdose on the ferry *Tor Brittania*, the largest ferry on the North Sea at that time. The weather was gin clear and there was a full moon shining. I couldn't have asked for an easier introduction to night winching! The crew had prepared the casualty on the lowest aft deck. It made for easy winching and my cockpit was level with a bar and terrace two decks up. I was watching the passengers drinking beer and raising their glasses to us as I kept a steady hover. As Steve was getting the stretcher ready to lift, one of the crew handed him a plastic bag which said, 'This is from the Captain to our favourite helicopter crew'. Steve held on to it as I got an 'Up gently' from Graham and we lifted Steve and the stretcher safely into the cabin. We took him to Great Yarmouth hospital. After unloading, Steve inspected the plastic bag which contained 400 cigarettes and two bottles of Scotch! Thank you, Captain!

On shift at Leconfield, on the first of April and in the afternoon, we heard traffic on the marine radio. A fishing vessel had suffered engine failure and was drifting. Not a job for us, as the position he gave meant that Humber lifeboat could take him under tow, even though the wind and swell were moving him westwards towards the coast. However, he was not at the position he had given, and the lifeboat couldn't see him when they got there. We were scrambled and Uncle Ron started talking to the skipper. It turned out that he was much closer to the coast than he had thought and was drifting towards the sea wall at Mablethorpe. It was nip and tuck if we could get to him. On the radio I heard, 'We are bouncing on the seabed, approaching the wall, how far away are you'! Ron replied, 'Five minutes Skipper, just five minutes.' Then, 'We're breaking up!' When we arrived, the boat was matchwood. The debris was washing against the concrete wall and the bodies of the crew were floating amongst it. There was nothing we could do, it was too dangerous to put Eric down to retrieve the bodies, so we left the scene.

I was devastated, it hit me hard that we had been too late but in those days before satellite navigation it was not unusual for positions to be wrong. The Coastguard had made the correct call tasking the lifeboat, it was a disaster which had started with a small error and escalated. Back at base, Eric took me to one side and told me to forget this loss, put it behind me and concentrate on the rest of the shift. He could see how angry I was but there was still a job to do. Old school counselling!

I was selected to be the display pilot for 1983. The boss must have thought my agricultural handling and lunatic torque turns were what people wanted to see. I had to work out a display routine which also involved a simulated rescue: winching a survivor from a one-man dinghy pinned to the ground. The Wessex didn't lend itself to anything too spectacular with its fully articulated rotor head, torque turns looked good though, pulling the nose up to almost vertical then squeezing up on the collective while leaving the pedals, would swing the nose around until you were pointing at the ground, then pull out of the dive. On 20 April my Giants Causeway pilot, Roy Citrine, was giving an impromptu display to some hikers in Snowdonia, when his Gazelle impacted the ground and disintegrated, killing him and his student. Just confirming the need to work up slowly and practise often before displaying.

Search and Rescue

On 25 April the boss came to Leconfield with an Air Marshal, the Commander of the Northern Maritime Region (COMNORMAR), to give the OK to my display routine. He then informed me that I would be displaying for Her Majesty the Queen and the Duke of Edinburgh during their visit to RAF Coltishall in ten days' time! I was honoured, flabbergasted and nervous all at the same time. Our display kicked off the proceedings and had to be finished exactly on time, as two squadrons of the station's Jaguars were screaming in for a mock airfield attack.

The next week was spent putting everything together and letting the Jaguar blokes know that I would be on the ground as they ran in! My last move was a 'bow' to the royal visitors before dashing back to our pan. At the planning meeting, there was a discussion as to whether aircrew, when meeting the royals, would be wearing hats or not. It was decided that hats would not be worn. This was overturned the day before the display and my crew of Eric and Uncle Ron advised me that they had not brought their hats, believing they were not required. Admittedly, we weren't walking around the station when off duty, but how two long-in-the-tooth Warrant Officers could not have uniform hats with them was incredible to me! Stores didn't have any so there was no alternative. We had to fly back to Leconfield to get two hats. Our flight commander there was Flt Lt Adrian Rule, and he had some words for the two old goats when we arrived!

67

Up Gently

The big day arrived at Coltishall, the Jaguars were all lined up facing each other on each side of the pan. The Queen's Flight aircraft arrived and parked at the far end, then the Queen and Prince Philip each took a line of Jaguars to walk along before meeting up in front of our Wessex, which was parked at the other end of the Jaguar lines. Her Majesty walked straight up to me, the Station Commander introduced her to me, and I gave my smartest salute and bowed. Standing behind her now were the Duke and the CAS With the Station Commander. She spoke with me for a while, and I can't remember a thing that was said! I introduced her to Eric, Uncle Ron and the engineers, who were stood smartly to attention (with hats). She asked Eric if he was nervous when he was dangling on the wire. He replied, 'Not half as nervous as I am now Ma'am'! From that day on he was known as the Royal Dangler. The Duke and CAS remembered me from Middle Wallop the year before (or they'd been well briefed) and we had a conversation about that time as Her Majesty was chatting with the engineers. Ron couldn't take his eyes off the massive scarab brooch she was wearing! The Royal party moved on to meet the families on the station and the aircraft were prepared for the display.

The display went perfectly, an engineer in the dinghy popped a flare and we ran in to rescue him. Once he was on-board, I commenced my hooligan antics in front of the Royal Dais, finishing with pointing towards them, slow

Search and Rescue

The author presents his crew to the Queen.

backwards movement before dipping the nose for the bow. Seconds ticking down now, so, racked it over to the right and hurried over to the SAR pan, landing just as the first attack appeared with mock explosions. After shutdown we climbed out and there were handshakes and grins all around (we didn't 'high five' in those days). It was the best day of my life so far! The subsequent photographs of us with the Queen

Ready for inspection.

were avidly shared with all of our families. I know that my Mum was about to burst with pride when she saw them. Dad was pleased too.

For the rest of that summer, I was giving displays at coastal lifeboat days, local events and major airfield displays, interspersed with shift work involving routine rescues, e.g., people cut off by the tide, cliff fallers, injured ship's crew, and inflatables drifting out to sea.

I was on shift, reading the *RAF News* one day. There was an article about the service starting to accept female pilots. I passed the good news onto my crew, prompting the winchman to say, 'It makes no odds to us John, just a different sort of cunt up front!'

On 26 August we were scrambled to reports of a Lightning crash at Scarborough. It was Friday, at the start of a bank holiday weekend and the beaches were packed. The Lightning had been doing a low-level display and had flipped and crashed into the North Bay. When we arrived, a coastguard was on scene, and he informed us that a small boat had recovered the body of the pilot. We asked him to clear some of the beach so that we could land to take the body on board. With the help of the police, he did this, bar one stubborn family who refused to move! We came in to land on the cleared area anyway and I think this family regretted their decision to stay. They were sandblasted! We ended up taking the pilot back to RAF Binbrook, the Lightning base. Six days later we flew the board of inquiry up to Scarborough for an airborne recce then back to Leconfield. It turned out that the pilot had been heading north to an official display but had agreed to give an impromptu display on the way, for some mates. He had misjudged a turn towards Scarborough Castle, pulled too hard and g-stalled, dropping into the sea. Shame.

Following a request from Humberside Fire Service, we trained some fire officers in winching from the helicopter. It came in very useful almost immediately. On 11 September, the ferry *Norwave* suffered an engine room fire departing Hull. She was still in the mouth of the Humber estuary but with no power. Of course, it was night time and blowing a gale! We scrambled to the Hull pickup point to collect two firemen and their equipment. The ship had her anchor down and thick black smoke was billowing from the funnel and being whipped aft by the gale. There was a small deck space clear of the smoke and Uncle Ron talked me in, getting the two firemen safely onto the deck. It was deemed that evacuation of the ship was not required, so we returned to base.

The next morning, I received a phone call, from a bloke calling himself the 'Treasury Solicitor'. He'd been reading his *Daily Telegraph* and the *Norwave* story had made the front page. It turned out that he was claiming salvage on behalf of the Ministry of Defence and, as Captain of the first asset to put a rescue line on board (with two firemen), I would be receiving a payout. Not for the value of the ship, I should add, as he was only claiming costs for the rescue, but it was at the salvage court's discretion to pay a bounty. As it turned out, this bounty was £1,200! I decided, of course, to split it three ways with my crew, Uncle Ron and Sgt Terry Williamson, the winchman. They agreed that we would fund a party in the hangar, free booze and food. The Squadron Commander disagreed, not Robin, we had a new guy, Sqn Ldr Roberts. He said that I was to share the bounty equally amongst all Squadron members. It would have worked out at a ridiculously small sum to each person. I checked with my Treasury Solicitor, and he assured me that the Squadron boss had no say in the matter, it was up to me. And so, the party went ahead!

December came around and we had a request to stand in for the Leuchars Wessex as they were having their Christmas party on the 7th. I flew our second Wessex up with Uncle Ron and MALM Dave Allen to cover the shift overnight.

Search and Rescue

Phantom aircraft were based there and one of the Squadrons was Number 43, 'The Fighting Cocks'. Ron had been on 43 as a young navigator on Meteors in the 50's. During the night, as Dave and I slept, Ron snuck out with a pot of paint and altered 43 Sqn's sign outside their hangar. No longer 'The Fighting Cocks', they were now 'The Farting Cooks'! Their Sqn Cdr was livid and initially blamed the other Phantom squadron on base. There was hell on with the Station Commander getting involved. Ron confessed to the two of us late in the day and I decided to leave for Leconfield ASAP! The old bugger laughed like a drain all the way home.

New Years Eve, and there was a party in the hangar. I was off duty until 08:00 the next day, along with my crewmembers. We agreed to see the New Year in with a couple of beers before midnight, to respect the eight hours 'bottle to throttle' rule, which was a joke, as we know. 2am came and we were still there, still with drinks. I realised the frank idiocy I was committing and headed to bed in the pilot's room. Sod's law followed again, and I was woken by the Scramble Bell just after eight! I struggled into my flying gear joined by the other two sheepish looking blokes. A fisherman had fallen at Bempton cliffs. Now, those cliffs are 300 feet high, so we didn't hold out much hope, but it turned out that there was a ladder to the bottom that fishermen took to reach the beach and he had only fallen the last thirty feet or so. Off we went, my blood alcohol letting me know that I wasn't operating at 100%. On arrival we saw that there was a small amount of beach. I could get us in at the bottom of the cliff, but it was close, and the wind meant that I was hovering left side to the cliff, looking across the cockpit. My eyes were like organ stops and I was sweating as we inched further left to get the winchman and stretcher down. The fisherman had injured his back, so he was strapped to a Neil Robertson stretcher, and we winched him in and took him to Scarborough hospital. The three of us were very relieved when we got back to base in one piece. The one and only time I went flying over the limit and I don't recommend it!

There was a force eleven gale on 13 January, equivalent to a force one Hurricane. A Belgian trawler, *Zeepaard*, was reported missing between Scarborough and Whitby, well offshore. Compatriot fishing vessels had chosen to shelter in Filey Bay. Sadly, ourselves and the Boulmer Sea King found no trace. All five on board had perished. It had been difficult just to get airborne!

Going through my logbook, it shows a quiet few months. There was a night winching job in April, lifting the Master of a small coaster, the *Lizzonia*, to Grimsby hospital. Flt Lt Mark Hewitt was the winch operator, and I don't think I had a better, calmer set of instructions in all my flying. Eric was on the wire—he seemed to be with me on all the best jobs! Otherwise, it was routine training and, once again, preparing for the display season and being checked out by COMNORMAR so he could allow me to perform in front of the public. There were two big airshows that year, Humberside Airport and RAF Church

Search and Rescue

Fenton, plus lifeboat days, fetes and flypasts. I was as happy as a sandboy.

We flew up to Leuchars again in August to cover a shift while they had their summer ball. Ron didn't come with us this time! The clock was ticking down to my leaving date, so I was relishing every flight. September passed with just a couple of minor jobs, then we were into October and the *Viscaria* Rescue on the 20th (chapter one). On the 28th we had a night scramble to lift an injured crewman from a rig support vessel. When we arrived overhead, there was a helideck raised up over the prow. I had never landed on a vessel before, but it made sense to do it rather than winch the casualty up. So, I asked the skipper to take a heading which was downwind and downswell, making my approach into wind. I judged the right moment over the deck and plonked her down! Great! Eric was able to lift the stretcher on board with the help of the crew. I picked the right time at the top of the swell for lift-off, then we were on our way to Hull Royal Infirmary. It was the first of many deck landings I would make in the future.

November was my last month in the RAF, and it turned out to be my busiest for rescues. On shift on the 13th we heard a Lightning call 'Mayday', and the pilot ejected just off the east coast. We scrambled immediately and homed onto the pilot's emergency beacon, getting overhead the ditching fifteen minutes after the call. We could see the fuel slick and our homer told us we were in exactly the right place. But we couldn't see the pilot. I came down to 300 feet and we traversed the crash site, searching. We were looking for his one-man dinghy, which should have stood out like the proverbial, but there was nothing. So frustrating as we knew he was very close. Eventually, Adrian Rule saw him, just his head showing above the waves, he was floating very low in the water, despite his life jacket. Adrian talked me round, into wind, Terry Williamson went out on the wire and got the strop round him. With an 'Up gently' Adrian winched them in, and it was obvious that the pilot's survival suit had leaked and was full of water. He had become separated from his dinghy on ejecting and wouldn't have lasted much longer. They got him to lie down in the cabin and he was so cold he was bouncing on the stretcher! We took him to Binbrook, but the MO there asked us to transfer him to Addenbrooke's hospital for recovery, which we did.

Five days later we lifted a trawler skipper fishing off Flamborough Head, into Scarborough hospital. Then, on the 19th, a Bristow Helicopters Bell 212 crashed into the sea at night, departing from an exploration rig, the *Cecil Provine*. It was a clear night, gentle wind and low sea state. We conducted a search, finding an upturned survival raft but it was empty. There were no survivors. I was looking towards the rig, giving me a reference in the hover. As we flew away, I banked left, losing sight of the rig, and started to experience a phenomenon known as 'The Leans'. I had the feeling that we were continuing to roll left, and it took all of my concentration to look at the artificial horizon, believe what it was telling me, then roll level and pull power to climb away from the sea. Otherwise, there would have been two helicopters ditching that night! It was a scary experience.

My last scramble was to a glider crash near Sutton Bank gliding club. It was on a steep bank and Adrian winched Eric down to where the pilot was still strapped in his cockpit. Once released, we winched him up and took him to Northallerton hospital. The landing site was on a grass quadrangle and after we had shut down and unloaded the starboard main wheel slowly started sinking into the grass. They had dug a drainage ditch and inserted a pipe across the grass without telling us! It stopped sinking and I reckoned I could start it and move to hard ground. Now, the Wessex was well known for suffering from a phenomenon known as 'Ground Resonance', where an interaction between the rotors and undercarriage can cause a vibration which can rip everything apart. That's why power was always applied before releasing the rotor brake, to accelerate the rotors as quickly as possible through the danger rpm. I got both engines started, applied power and released the brake, ready to pull some pitch even when winding up! She started OK but with a lot of wobble, and I moved a couple of yards to safe ground. I had got away with it but with hindsight and the wisdom of age, I should have waited for a bloody great crane to lift her out.

Up Gently

My last shift was on 30 November. I had a training trip and, on landing, the blokes had a yard of ale and a nice cigar ready for me, while another pilot took over the shift. My RAF days were over.

The author's last flight as an RAF pilot.

Chapter 5

Bond Helicopters

For helicopter pilots in the eighties, they said all roads lead to Aberdeen, and so it was for me. I ended up with a choice of going to the largest operator on the North Sea, Bristow Helicopters, or one of the smallest, Bond Helicopters. After my interview at Bond, it was easy to decide. There was a better atmosphere around the hangar, everyone knew everyone else, and promotion was done on merit. The interview was done by the Ops Manager, Trevor Larman, and the Chief Pilot, Bob Denning. Trevor was a straight-talking bloke, called a spade a fucking shovel and Bob seemed a very serious, capable manager. I liked both blokes and they liked me enough to take me on!

Training started in February 1985, and I took up a kind offer to stay—for those days I was there—with my Dad's Aberdeen relatives, Eleanor and Dave Craig. Days off would see me commuting back to Beverley, preparing to sell the house. I ended up staying far too long with the Craigs, they were so kind and generous, and, in the end, it must have been a pain having this glaikit pilot around the house! I can never thank them enough.

Super Puma

I was starting as a co-pilot at Bond, flying the Aérospatiale 332L Super Puma. Compared to the old Wessex, it was the starship *Enterprise*, modern in every sense. Our training Captain was Bob Bibby, who had an encyclopaedic knowledge of the 332 and had the hard task of drumming it into our heads, but he was the best ground school instructor I ever came across. Two others started with me that month, Steve Pyttlik and Mark 'Fatman' Barclay—I never did discover the origin of his nickname— possibly it was ironic, as he was pretty thin! The Super Puma carried 19 passengers; the maximum allowed without having a cabin attendant. Passengers were always referred to as the 'Bears', an affectionate term for anyone working on the rigs. The cockpit contained all of the instruments, radios and navigation equipment to allow the use of airways and to enter controlled airspace following Instrument Flight Rules (IFR). I held a Master Green military instrument rating but a civilian rating was in a different league. To begin with, in those days, co-pilots held a basic Visual Flight Rules licence but with a company instrument check, could fly with Captains who held a full Instrument Rating alongside their Airline

The Aérospatiale 332L Super Puma.

Transport Licence. So, Bob worked us up to a check ride and basic Instrument check.

I found that in the civilian world there was much more emphasis on single-engine safety. We always had to calculate our weight to be able to fly away or land safely with one engine failed, whereas in the military you would use the power available with two, all of the time. The Makila engines were powerful lumps but didn't like it when the airflow to the intake was less than ideal, such as when hovering downwind. In that case you could get a compressor stall when airflow reversed through it, making loud banging noises and reducing the power available. There was a button under the Collective Lever which opened a valve in the compressor casing, stopping the pressure build-up. You had to make sure it was selected on approach with the 'Offset' caption displayed, or the engine would remind you of its own accord! The autopilot was a wonderful piece of kit, fully coupled it reduced the workload considerably. You could get it to hold height, heading, and airspeed. It would also follow the navigation route you had selected or fly down the Instrument Landing System (ILS). Into the modern world!

After a month of training and check rides I was released to the line to fly as a competent co-pilot and began earning my keep. We were flying to permanent oilfields like the Forties, Magnus, Alwyn as well as the floating exploration rigs with exotic names like 'Sovereign Explorer', 'Treasure Swan', 'Ocean Nomad' and many others. Planning the trip was key. It was possible to reach the major fields in the East Shetland Basin directly from Aberdeen, using airfields on Shetland as diversions if needed. When the weather was not ideal, we could route via Sumburgh (on Shetland) or Kirkwall (Orkney) to top-up on fuel before continuing. There was a strict route structure using radials from a beacon at Scotstown Head, North of Aberdeen. With the latest weather information, crews could calculate the fuel required and pass a useable payload figure to the passenger terminal. Fuel required to return from the rigs to Aberdeen was a much simpler calculation as long as the weather was reasonable, otherwise diversion fuel to Inverness might be required. Once airborne there was a running calculation of fuel used, fuel required and minimum fuel at destination and/ or diversion. The weather played its part in one of the most hostile environments for helicopter flying and was often very different from the forecast!

As a co-pilot I found it interesting to see the differences among the captains. Although we had Standard Operating Procedures there were many different takes on these. On two occasions, with two different captains, I found myself agreeing to a very non-standard approach to a rig, when weather had deteriorated and the cloud base was below the minimum required. Normally, you would have the rig on your radar picture in the cockpit and, knowing the cloud base was a safe height above the helideck with a reasonable visibility, you would descend—in cloud—slowly towards it, breaking out of cloud and seeing it straight ahead. On these other occasions the cloud base was on the helideck, although visibility beneath was acceptable.

Rather than divert to Shetland we set up to approach the rig safety vessel. These were stationed by each rig and generally looked like retired trawlers. After identifying the vessel, an approach was started, keeping it on the radar. As we descended through the helideck level, we became visual with the vessel, and beyond it, the legs of the huge oil rig. We then hovered across towards those legs and began a vertical climb, up into the cloud base, ready to swing away from the rig if contact was lost, eventually reaching the helideck and moving across to land. Not a procedure I would recommend! Both Captains said that they would only have attempted it because they were confident in my experience and abilities. Rig radar approach procedures have tightened up considerably since then. The Bears on the rigs were very happy, of course, as they were heading home—all smelling of aftershave. The ones we discharged on the rig smelled of booze, even from the night before. They should have developed an autopilot which detected cabin smell. Booze, away from Aberdeen; Aftershave, towards Aberdeen!

I had the pleasure of flying with Trevor, the Ops Manager, in June. We were heading up to the west of Shetland—for a change—to the Sovereign Explorer rig. It was a two-hour trip to get there, and the Bears all settled in for a snooze. It was a beautiful day, blue skies and good visibility. We checked in with Shetland Radar who informed us that there was no traffic in our vicinity, so we continued on our way. Suddenly, there was a loud roar, audible over the noise of the helicopter even though we had earphones on! Two RAF F4 Phantoms were passing either side of us, from behind and close in. You could see they had flaps down and were hanging on their afterburners, making the racket. The Bears were all awake now! The Phantoms cleaned up and dove back to low-level. Trevor's language regarding Shetland Radar and RAF pilots was colourful, to say the least! Checked with Shetland again and they had not seen the encounter. I'm sure the Phantom crews had enjoyed their jolly jape.

I was back in Beverley in September for my wedding, at the Minster, to wife number 1. Then back to work and renting a cottage at a place called Little Ythsie. It was bloody cold and only a coal fire in the lounge!

My logbook shows that it was busy for the rest of the year, with much more flying than on SAR. For the first two months of 1986 my commercial trips were mixed with instrument flying training, working towards my instrument rating, a necessity to gain promotion to North Sea Commander. Bob, the Chief Pilot, took the training for me and 'Fatman' Barclay. I mentioned earlier that the civilian Instrument Rating was in a different league. Of special note here is the wonderful utility known as the holding procedure. This fiendish device is a racetrack oval, flown at a set speed, with a designated track to follow towards a beacon. You then turn left or right to turn onto a downwind heading, before turning into wind to pick up the inbound track. The whole oval must take *exactly* four minutes and your height and airspeed should not vary. Sounds easy? But you might be approaching the beacon from a different direction, meaning you have to manoeuvre to gain the inbound track. So you can have a direct join or (depending on what quadrant you are approaching from) the join can be offset or parallel. Then you need to factor in the wind and adjust your downwind leg for drift and groundspeed.

It's a constant stream of mental arithmetic. Meanwhile, your examiner might simulate an engine fire/hydraulic problem/fuel leak/ electrical emergency! Two approaches have to be flown, one using the Instrument Landing System and one (non-precision) using a beacon with track and time calculated to the airfield. Flying on a designated airway is also part of the test. It was hard work for Bob getting us up to a standard which would be acceptable to the CAA. The big day finally came on 5 March. Our examiner was Capt. Don Sissons, a respected name in the helicopter world. Bob remained our co-pilot with Don on the jump seat. Fat Man took the first trip, departing Aberdeen down the airway to Edinburgh with me as passenger, sweating in the cabin. Then a crew change, and I was to fly us back to Aberdeen. Once settled in, I took control and lifted from Edinburgh straight into a holding procedure followed by a non-precision approach and go-around, joining the airway to fly back to Aberdeen. We were flying above a solid layer of cloud which was about 300 feet below us. As we passed north of Perth suddenly US Air Force F 1-11s were punching through the cloud all around going almost vertical past us! Fatman was out of his seat, heading to the cockpit to warn us, but Bob and Don were already aware. Don said, 'Forget the test, maximum climb. *Now!*' I complied, pulling maximum pitch and reducing speed towards 70 knots. Radar were warning us of the traffic at the same time that we saw them, then the Americans checked in, apologised to radar, and said that they had to abort a low level training trip due to weather. We were bloody lucky that none of them had hit us. The Americans had been training for a raid on Libya which took place a few weeks later. Don filed an air miss report and we continued towards my instrument approach to Aberdeen, which went well and I passed the test, as did Fatman. We enjoyed a couple of beers that evening!

I had had good advice from Capt. Steve Duffy beforehand. He had told me to make sure that my shoes were polished. 'How will that help me'? I asked. 'Because when it's all going to rat shit and you are lost around the beacon, you can look at your shoes and know they are shinier than his'! It made me laugh and relieved the stress a bit anyway.

So now I had the grand title of Senior First Officer, with three gold bars on my shoulder to replace the two. The next couple of months were spent flying routine trips to the rigs. In late May, I had an enjoyable trip accompanying Capt. Raz Zoers, driving down to the company base at Bourn airfield in Cambridgeshire, to collect our new Super Puma, G-PUMI. We spent a couple of days flying acceptance air tests, then flew up to Blackpool airfield, another Bond base servicing the Irish Sea gas rigs with Dauphin helicopters. It was great to be away from Aberdeen, seeing a bit of the countryside!

The next day we flew two trips out to the gas rigs, ferrying VIPs back and forward, then departed for Aberdeen on the following day. I really enjoyed the trips with Raz, who was a line training Captain, and it hopefully reinforced my request for a promotion to Captain. I believe it did because, four weeks after that trip, I was flying as Captain under supervision, leading to command if my performance was up to scratch. I had eight days of being assessed, one in particular was noteworthy on 1 July. I was crewed with Capt. Guthrie Young, a gentleman of the old school and an ex-RAF pilot. He had previously flown for Bristow but had been a victim of redundancies there at some point in the past. He disliked Bristow intensely.

On this day, a request had come in to fly to the Thistle rig in the East Shetland Basin. This was normally a Bristow contract but, due to fog in the field, they had grounded all flights to rigs in that area. I took a look at the weather and decided that we could start making headway towards the rig as I reckoned that the fog would burn off. If it didn't, we had fuel enough to divert to Unst, on Shetland, as it was gin clear there. Bond left decisions to individual Captains whereas Bristow had a more blanket approach. So, to Guthrie's great delight, we taxied across the airfield in our bright red Bond aircraft, through the ranks of stationary Bristow machines, to park outside the Bristow terminal and collect their passengers. As we headed north, weather updates showed that the fog was thinning and as we entered the basin we could see the Thistle platform. I had estimated correctly, and the fog had gone! One set of Bears was swapped for aftershave Bears and we headed south. At Aberdeen we again taxied to the Bristow terminal to dislodge our happy passengers before heading across the runway to Bond. Guthrie was beaming and I guess my write-up for that day was pretty good.

Eventually, I was put forward for a Captain's base check with the formidable Bob Bibby. A flight test covering every emergency you could think of, then the rest of the day in the flight planning room where he picked my brain on every subject. Some answers I was required to know immediately, others I had to know where to find the information. It was a gruelling day but, at the end, Bob confirmed that I had reached the required standard, and I was awarded my four gold bars by Declan Dawson, the Ops Supervisor who addressed me with my new title for the first time, 'Congratulations Captain!'

The next day's crewing had already been arranged, so I found myself still co-piloting with Keith Copus. It wasn't until the day after that I was in command, my first co-pilot being an ex-RAF friend who had joined Bond after me, Frank Pole. A much more experienced pilot in years and hours, so it made my first day very comfortable. However, Frank is the first to admit that he had a bit of finger trouble on departure, and we were out of contact with ATC for a minute or two! Otherwise, a smooth trip to the 'Safe Felicia' and back, when the only time I pulled rank was in first choice of the cakes which came on board from the rig galley! Then I had three days flying with my good friend, Pete Hogston, who lived in the same town as me, Ellon. It made for a relaxed, but professional, cockpit environment. Talking of which, I volunteered to take part in a North

Up Gently

Sea cockpit environment study being conducted by Westland Helicopters.

For three days I was crewed with the same copilot, Mike Hayler, and we were wired up to a portable device for the whole time which monitored pulse and body core temperature (don't ask where the probe went). On each flight we had a young lady sitting on the jump seat, taking notes of everything we said, did and consumed. On the last flight, returning to Aberdeen after a long day, there was maintenance work on the runway, and we were to land on the taxiway. I don't know if Mike was tired or stressed but he continued towards the runway. I reminded him of the change, but he was getting very low, so I took control and jinked to the left to land on the taxiway. I'd love to have known what my stress parameters showed then! I never did hear the results of the survey which was done with multiple crews in different companies.

Bus driving to the rigs and back continued, but the next month (September), I was tasked with a trip down to East Yorkshire to collect VIPs from the onshore gas facility at Easington and take them to rig 8A in the Rough field (my refuel rig in chapter one). It was only a stone's throw from Leconfield, so I asked Bob Denning if he wouldn't mind if I called in there, and he agreed. My copilot for the day was 'Sparky' Harden, an ex-Royal Navy pilot who had recently joined Bond. A real character who was a natural pilot but also an adrenalin junkie! He was an avid skydiver who knew no fear. We took along a Bond girl,

Karen, as cabin crew for our VIPs. I gave Sparky the flying for the outbound trip to Leconfield. With no passengers on board his departure from Aberdeen was spirited and definitely not the standard take-off, to the point that Air Traffic asked us if everything was alright!

Arriving at Leconfield involved a low-level beat-up across the disused airfield, missing the Army vehicles on the runways. Then a wing-over to land on the pan. It was great to meet my old mates and show them what a modern helicopter was like! I had also arranged for my in-laws to be there and let them get on board. As it turned out, we had plenty of time before heading to Easington, so with the collusion of Sparky and Karen, I gave them a five-minute flight around Beverley, with my brother-in-law on the jump seat—another adrenalin junkie as he raced motorcycle sidecars! Bob had definitely not agreed to that!

With the in-laws discharged, we headed off to Easington with Sparky flying. En route, the visibility was not great, hazy with maybe one mile visible. We were flying at 1,000 feet and suddenly, on my side, I saw a fast jet at the same height on a converging course. With no time to call it I just grabbed the cyclic and collective, yelled 'Jet!', and pushed down, the Jet pulled up and went over our heads. It had been close. I subsequently filed an air miss report and discovered that it was a Phantom out of Coningsby on a pilot training trip. The front seat pilot hadn't seen us, but the rear seater had and pulled up. With our closing speed I reckon we had six or seven seconds to avoid each other. Throw in the 'Startle' effect and we were lucky.

We arrived at Easington a few minutes later and boarded our VIPs. I took the flying for my gentle captain's leg out to the rig. We got the passengers off and I gave it to Sparky to fly us, empty, back to Easington. Again, he was enjoying himself as he lifted and moved forward, pushing the nose almost vertically down off the 100-foot helideck, pulling out at wavetop height and returning to Easington. I knew Sparky would be up to these shenanigans but didn't feel the need to rein him in. He was a good pilot, and I was enjoying the ride. I flew the return to Aberdeen in a more relaxed manner. Next day Sparky and I were back to bus driving to the Safe Felicia.

There was a major design problem with the Puma/Super Puma/EC225 cockpits as far as I was concerned. There were two 'T' handles, both in the floor between the pilots, one locked the nose wheel in the fore/aft position, the other applied the handbrake to the main wheels. They were different colours but mounted close together. You could pull up the nosewheel lock as you were turning, and it would click into the lock when you straightened up. It had to be locked for take-off. One day, we were late for departure having had an unserviceable aircraft and swapping to another. It was teeming with rain and as we entered the runway and I was turning to line up, I called for the nosewheel lock. Sod's law, my copilot pulled the wrong handle and the main wheels locked, making us skid sideways! Thank goodness the runway was wet or there could have been a different outcome. I know from other pilots that this was not an isolated occurrence, Aérospatiale really should have changed the arrangement.

That has reminded me of another rushed departure after changing aircraft. We rattled through the checks, lined up and completed the departure checks when my copilot, Terry Mcloughlin, asked me if I was going to strap in. I was sitting with my straps hanging loose! Too busy to buckle up! Needless to say, I quickly did.

1987 arrived and I was enjoying my flying, although it could be repetitive at times, back and forwards to the Alwyn platform. Since the day I joined Bond, I had had my sights set on one particular job, Senior Pilot/SAR Pilot based offshore on the Forties field, and I started nagging Trevor about it at every opportunity. It was to pay off at the end of the year. Meanwhile, I continued flying the 332L. I had a check ride in January and then renewed my instrument rating in April in the simulator over at Bristow. A very rudimentary affair compared with today's machines, the cockpit windows were opaque but all the dials and knobs inside worked!

In May, I developed appendicitis and had to have it removed. I was away from flying for four weeks so had a quick check with a training Captain, Mike Todd, in June. My parents came to visit in July, and I got Bob Denning to allow my father to fly jump seat with me and Andy

Busby on a trip to the Safe Felicia. It was great to show him what went on. He was always an avid photographer, chairman of the local photography club but, on this trip, he forgot his camera! My Mum was livid when we got back home. The long summer days of Northern Scotland continued, and I was racking up plenty of flying. Still nagging Trevor at every opportunity for the Forties Field position.

October came and with it I was handed an interesting task, to take a Super Puma to the Blackpool base and fly some Conservative MPs out to the gas rigs in the Irish Sea. The Conservative Party conference was being held in Blackpool that year and the boss was obviously currying favour with them. Steve Potton was my copilot, an ex-Army pilot with a good sense of humour which made for an enjoyable couple of days. On the first day we flew a group of 19 MPs, suitably briefed and attired in their survival suits. I don't know if they were nervous, but they were a noisy lot, chattering and shouting in the cabin. We returned, empty, to Blackpool to wait while they were shown around before returning to pick them up again. The next day we were to fly the Energy Minister, Cecil Parkinson, plus his entourage, to visit the gas field. He had been involved in a scandal previously, having had an affair with his secretary. The press just seemed to want a picture of him in his rubber survival suit, but the operations staff managed to keep them away! It was the same procedure as the previous day, fly to the rig, drop the VIPs, then return to Blackpool to await the call to pick them up. Eventually we landed back at Blackpool to finish the task. Steve stepped out of the cockpit and opened the main cabin door where Mr Parkinson disembarked saying, 'Thank you, well done!' Steve subsequently became the Chief Pilot at Blackpool but was to die in a crash approaching the gas rigs—at night—many years later.

Later that month Steve and I flew fixed wing across to Bergen to collect a Super Puma which had diverted there due to weather. It wasn't unusual to nominate Norwegian airfields as weather diversions from the East Shetland Basin. Unfortunately, the weather at Aberdeen was just as bad and we spent two nights in the Sumburgh Hotel on Shetland. Think 'Star Wars' bar and you are getting close!

My nagging now paid off and Trevor called me in to tell me that I would be changing to the Dauphin fleet (Aérospatiale 365N) and appointed Senior Pilot on the Forties Field for BP, working week on/week off. The Dauphin was used as the in-field shuttle for the five rigs there and was based on the 'Iolair' floating rig used for diving support and firefighting. It had a small hangar which would take the Dauphin with blades folded but, generally, the helicopter was parked outside. The facility was declared as a Search And Rescue unit to the Rescue Coordination Centre at Pitreavie and there were two SAR crewmen based offshore at all times. Only the Senior Pilot was tasked for SAR callouts, so my background was perfect for the job. Another bonus was that it was probably the best paid position in the company! Trevor had one last request. Sparky had been promoted to Captain and would be joining me on the Forties Dauphin. He wanted me to keep an eye on him and try to wind in any hooligan tendencies! There was never any need to say a word of course, Sparky was an accomplished pilot. As I write this, 34 years on from that conversation, Sparky is still flying and saving lives as a HEMS pilot in the USA.

Dauphin

I started training on the Dauphin in December, at the company base at Strubby, a disused WW2 airfield in Lincolnshire. The Dauphins there serviced the mid-North Sea gas rigs. The Dauphin was a delight; sleek, modern and fast with the same autopilot as the Super Puma but an upgrade to the navigation equipment called SARnav. For SAR the passenger seats could quickly be removed and a pallet carrying the SAR equipment bolted in while the engineers attached the electric winch. My trainer was an experienced ex-Navy pilot called Alan Rock. He could be a bit irascible and not a bloke to fool around with, but I liked his professionalism and safety ethos. He went on to be the first Chief Pilot for London HEMS when they started operations with a Dauphin. He checked me out for general handling, emergencies, and instrument rating, which was even more demanding as single pilot! Hard enough with a copilot to help out but

Bond Helicopters

Operating the Dauphin offshore.

totally demanding on your own. I then spent a week flying out of Great Yarmouth to the southern North Sea rigs for line training. Back up to Aberdeen and a couple of days being checked out for winching and use of the SARnav, into which you could enter a search pattern, couple the autopilot and the aircraft would fly itself, allowing you to keep eyes outside, searching, for much longer. The next day I launched on a single-pilot navigation exercise to deliver engineering equipment from Longside to the Iolair, then on to the Frigg field (another Dauphin base), before returning to Longside. Just me on board. Nobody to argue with for first choice of the cakes!

I then began my offshore life. I spent the first week working alongside my opposite number as Senior Pilot, Ptolly Mortimer, getting to know the operation. Our SAR training Captain, Phil

Up Gently

Fisher came out for a couple of days to witness some deck winching with the safety vessel, 'Stonehaven'. (We nicknamed Phil 'Philly the Fish' after the fish/goalkeeper in Viz). Then settled into a steady week on/week off routine, flying back and forward to the field as a passenger on a Bristow S61. The in-field shuttle ran three times each day, one for each pilot offshore. Most of the time I was with Sparky and a ridiculously young-looking bloke, Marcus Griffiths, 'Griffo', who had gained his licence the hard way, starting out as a crop sprayer and progressing to North Sea Commander. We had some good laughs along with our two engineers, John Dunlop and Brian, also our crewmen who were mainly ex-Royal Navy. I would schedule a SAR training trip each Sunday morning with various exercises including deck winching and drums. After which, as Senior Pilot, I would fly as a passenger across to the Alpha rig for a weekly meeting with the BP field manager to discuss the operation in his grand office, followed by Sunday lunch in the Alpha canteen. The offshore catering was world-class, and I was happy to indulge! Even the food on the Iolair was high-standard and I certainly didn't lose weight working offshore. I had a couple of SAR medevacs from floating facilities, one in March, a broken jaw case we took to the Bravo rig. Then, in May, a heart attack victim who we took to Aberdeen Royal Infirmary.

I was as happy as a sandboy. But then, back in April, our crewman Alex Knight was reading the *Aberdeen Press and Journal* and told me that there was a job advertisement that might interest me. It read: 'A private operator wishes to recruit a tenth pilot for a varied operation in a pleasant part of the Middle East. The appointed pilot would hold an ATPL/H or equivalent, with a minimum of 2,500 hours I/C helicopters, the majority twin turbine. An instrument rating is essential, an instructor rating desirable. Previous military experience is considered essential, with a leavening of commercial time. Puma/Super Puma experience is highly desirable, although the pilot may not have the type on his licence at present. Previous ME experience would be advantageous but, above all, we require a flexible attitude, an adaptable personality, and a sense of humour. In return we offer a very attractive tax-free salary, free accommodation, power and water, with free local phone calls. This is an accompanied vacancy, sixty days paid leave p. a., normally in two periods of one month, travel at company's expense. Education allowance is paid. Initial contract is for two years, renewable yearly thereafter. A 20% gratuity is paid after two years and yearly thereafter.'

I was intrigued and sent off an application. I was selected for interview at the Airport Marriott shortly afterwards along with many others. The interview was conducted by two ex-RAF pilots, Jim Cheetham and Duncan Donaldson, Chief Pilot and deputy Chief Pilot respectively, of the Royal Flight of Oman. This information was only given when the interview commenced! It went very well, Duncan remembered me from 72 Sqn days, especially a night flying brief I had given for multiple Squadrons which was thorough and comprehensive. He had told me so at the time. I had thanked him and asked him to pass it on to my boss! Wages were not mentioned until the very end and not until I asked about them. I nearly fell off my chair. It was double what I was currently earning, plus it was tax-free with those 20% gratuities added on! I was delighted when they rang me later, at home, to tell me that I had the job, subject to security clearance. When that was done, I could give my three months' notice to Bond.

So now I knew that my life was about to change, again, but continued to enjoy the job on the Forties. My clearance arrived at the start of June, and I immediately handed my notice to Trevor. He was not too happy of course, he'd given me the job I wanted, now I was off. He told me I'd get fed up being at the beck and call of the Sultan but could see the attraction of the wages! I discovered, later on, that Bob Bibby had actually been with the Royal Flight in the late seventies, but he didn't speak of it to me. Only that I should go and enjoy it. Typical Bob.

6 July 1988 was a dreadful date on the North Sea. Just after 10pm, through human error, there was a series of massive explosions on the Piper Alpha rig, destroying it completely. 167 men lost their lives that night. I heard the news the next morning as I was preparing for my week offshore. The mood was grim at the Bristow terminal as we boarded the S61 for the trip to the Iolair, which

Bond Helicopters

had motored north in the night to be available for firefighting if needed. I imagined that I would be hearing tales from Ptolly and the guys about what they had been up to overnight, but they were not happy. The Rescue Coordination Centre had not even considered them and only scrambled military resources, RAF Sea Kings from Leuchars and Boulmer. The Boulmer aircraft had to actually overfly the Iolair to get to Piper Alpha! Our Dauphin would have been first on scene, a whole hour ahead of the first Sea King. The RAF crews did a magnificent job, as always, but forever there will be the thought that a rescue helicopter available one hour before they arrived might have made a difference. Maybe not, but they should have been given a chance. I spent the rest of the day flying search patterns around the remains of Piper Alpha looking, looking, looking for any survivors in the sea but there were none.

Just a few weeks later I was off to my new job.

Chapter 6

Oman

In 1988 Oman was still a remote and exotic country. Sultan Qaboos had deposed his father in 1970 and had started to invest the country's great oil wealth into transforming an almost stone age country into a modern nation. A Muslim country but very tolerant and pro-west, an important ally in the Middle East, the Sultan had been educated at Sandhurst. He was keen that all his citizens had access to education and health care, and that girls had the same opportunities as boys. He spent most of his time at a Palace called Bait Al Barka, situated to the west of Seeb (Muscat) Airport, the base airport for the Royal Flight. He had other palaces around the country, Jalali Palace in Old Muscat, Sohar Palace on the coast 120 miles to the west, and three palaces in the south of the country at Salalah, Al Husn, Robat and Mamurah.

This is the Dhofar region of Oman where, in the summer months of July, August and September, there is a microclimate caused by the south-west monsoon and the local topography which creates low cloud and rain with lower temperatures. So, he would spend those months there, usually staying at Mamurah. That is where he was when I arrived in country. I had a couple of weeks in Muscat to get the wife settled into the Royal Flight housing complex and complete the admin requirements. Then I flew down to Salalah on the Sultan's 747, to join the Royal Flight helicopter detachment based in a hangar at Robat Palace.

There were three VIP helicopters: two AS332C, the same Super Puma spec as on the North Sea but with a shorter Puma-sized fuselage, and one SA330J Puma. There were also three 330J helicopters in military configuration for Royal Guard tasking. The VIP aircraft had luxury interiors, of course, with gold and gold-plated fixtures and fittings on upholstered seats. They could take ten passengers, four in a forward compartment and six in smaller seats in the rear cabin. All the helicopters were painted in camouflage, even though they were civilian-registered. There had been a war with Yemeni rebels in the Dhofar region since the early seventies and it had not long finished. There was still a threat when flying near the border, so it was avoided.

I was straight into some intensive training and scrutiny from the training pilots John Nowell and Bill Burborough, neither of whom I warmed to. The important thing was just to prove my ability, something which I was happy to do, and I began by renewing my type and instrument rating on the 332C, for the issue of my Omani ATPL(H). Training for operations followed, including deck landings on the Sultan's yacht, HMRY *Al Said*, in preparation for his return to Muscat that month, which he would do by sea. I was impressed by the slick procedures in place for VIP tasks, including coordinated shutdowns, when all helicopters would stop their rotors at exactly the same time.

I've mentioned the Chief pilot and deputy, Jim and Duncan, as well as the trainers. The other three ex-RAF blokes were Phil Todd (Toddy), Baz Longhurst and Pete Norton. Three great guys who were good company at all times. Toddy especially, enjoyed a beer or two, and I was happy to join him. Our other two pilots were an Aussie—Phil Stevens—a Vietnam Vet with the straightforward Australian outlook on life, and an ex-British Army chap, Nick Mylne. He had flown Skeeters in the Dhofar war and had stayed on in Oman, eventually starting up the Royal Flight helicopter unit, and had actually given flying lessons to the Sultan in the early days. Nick was a fluent Arabic speaker and a mine of information about Oman and the Omanis. He had a great sense of humour and was always good company.

We had six Omani crewmen, Saif, Saud, Moosa, Saad, Said and Mohammed. All ex-military and all experienced in the role. They would be taking care of troops onboard one day and serving heads of state on the VVIP aircraft the next. As with RAF crewmen, they were conversant in underslung load and winching tasks, helping with navigation and radios when sitting up front in the 330s.

HM (our usual term when talking about the sultan) sailed around the coast, returning to Muscat in October. We shadowed his movements, spending a couple of nights at the Sultan of Oman's Air Force (SOAF) airbase at Masirah on the way. We would be back in Muscat for a few days, and then HM would often decide to drive to his farm in Sohar. Whenever he drove any distance, the Royal Guard had us shadow the convoy with two VIP aircraft and two trooping 330s. Plus, there was always a Royal Oman Police (ROP) Bell 214ST with medics onboard. When he stayed in Sohar we had one 330 based at the ROP station in the town, on standby. I first flew the Sultan that month as copilot with Duncan as my Captain. HM decided to return to Muscat by helicopter, so we all positioned to the helipads at the farm. As copilot I stood outside the cockpit, to one side of the airstair door, with the crewman at the other side. As HM approached, we both saluted, and he returned the salute as he climbed onboard. His bodyguards would follow, then his guests or royal court members, with his slave (yes slave!) bringing up the rear carrying HM's gun and any bags. Once aboard I had to quickly close the cabin door as Duncan started the engines, then open the cockpit door, throw my hat in and pull myself up into the left-hand seat, and run quickly through the checklist. When we were running smoothly, the other helicopters started up and we lifted, heading along the coast to Muscat. One important point was to extinguish the seat belt sign as soon as possible, as he didn't like it on for too long!

By early January 1989 I was checked out on the 330J Puma and joined the full roster, 4 days VIP/2days escort with one day off standby. Most days were spent doing training trips to stay current. There was the odd task to transport government ministers or visiting VIPs, e.g. I flew the Austrian Defence Minister to Goat Island in the Straits of Hormuz. Quite what he was doing there, I don't know, but he seemed pleased with the trip! My first daughter was born that January, in the Royal Hospital, Muscat.

At the end of the month HM began one of his 'Meet the People' tours. These consisted of a huge convoy of vehicles heading out of Muscat, into the mountains and desert. This one was routing straight down the 600-mile main road, through the desert to Salalah. The helicopters were allotted positions above the convoy, two escort Pumas leading the way, close to HM's vehicle in the lead, followed by the ROP and the two VIP aircraft bringing up the rear. There were

Oman

*Oman's Sultan Qaboos bin Said was the Arab
world's longest-serving ruler.*

miles between the front and rear of the convoy!
At some point which suited him, HM would pull
off the road and all the vehicles would follow,
setting up a campsite which, in those days,
consisted of one large ring of tents and vehicles.
HM's tent was on one side with ministers either
side of him, the helicopter ops and engineering
wagons on the other side of the circle, with
helicopters parked close by. The commander of
the Royal Guard, General Geoff Harcort, always
made sure that the convoy only ran in daylight
hours, just in case we were needed, also to allow
safe landing at the new location. Harcort was
a strange character, a career soldier who was
very close to HM since the day that he usurped
his father and took control of the country. The
General was, in effect, our customer. Every task
we did came through the Royal Guard and had

to be sanctioned by him. He took a close interest in the helicopter section, and he made the Chief Pilot's life hell, calling him at all hours of day and night.

We all slept in pup tents under a camouflage net slung on the side of the ops wagon. It was an old Bedford four-tonner, with an air-conditioned cabin stuck on the back. There was a similar wagon for the engineers to keep all their stuff in. An old generator supplied the power for the wagons and some lighting and power to our cook tent. It was important to keep your tent zipped up, as unwelcome visitors could include scorpions, snakes or camel spiders. They could sometimes be heard scrabbling over your tent as you slept! I was handed the brief to purchase new vehicles for the convoy and ended up with Hino wagons from South Korea. The company built them exactly to my specification and convoys definitely improved from then on. Sometimes Ministers would visit to enjoy a cup of tea and sit in our air-conditioned comfort.

HM famously never married. He surrounded himself with courtiers of the Royal Court who were all handsome young men, living in his palaces wherever he went. We referred to them as HM's boys, although on one task, I learned a different name. I was flying with Toddy in the second VIP. The first VIP was briefed to carry HM plus others, while Toddy and I were told to take the 'Snooker Team'. I asked him what the hell that meant, he just said 'Wait and see'. We were all parked up and waiting as the vehicles arrived and disgorged their passengers. In the lead was HM and his followers, while bringing up the rear, and heading towards us, was a gaggle of multi-coloured dish-dashes, looking for all the world like Snooker balls! I couldn't help but laugh, controlling myself before they boarded.

1989 was a busy year for the Sultan, and for me! He stayed in Salalah in March. I returned to UK in April for my first month's leave, preparing the house for sale in Aberdeen. A couple of crewmen, Said and Moosa, were visiting Aberdeen that month for their dunker and fire training, so I took the blokes out on the town for a few beers. Most of the Omanis enjoyed a smoke and a drink in those pre-9/11 days. Moosa sported an impressive beer-belly, for sure! Back to Oman in May, where HM had flown north to Muscat. Then mid-June to mid-August he embarked on the *Al-Said* to cruise around the Mediterranean. We put two helicopters onto the *Fulk Al Salamah* support ship, tucked in the hangar, and we followed the *Al Said*, eventually visiting Gibraltar, crossing the Bay of Biscay and sailing into Southampton. The only flying we did was a couple of cross-decking trips to have lunch with the crew on the *Al Said*. From UK HM flew directly to Salalah, as the khareef (southeastern monsoon) was still in effect, and on return to Muscat we moved the operation down there.

HM flew back to Muscat in October, in preparation for a major state visit to the United Arab Emirates. He flew to Abu Dhabi in his Jumbo, then embarked on the *Al-Said* to visit each Emirate in turn. We flew the helicopters to Abu Dhabi on the same day, then on to Dubai, Sharjah, Ras Al Khaima and Fujairah as he visited each one. Duncan and I flew HM five days in a row, taking him from his yacht each day and returning him there in the evening. The first time I was the handling pilot I took him to a village which had opted to remain part of Oman when Borders were drawn, even though it was within the UAE! The locals were overjoyed to see him, and the Royal Guard had their hands full trying to keep them away from our helicopter as we started up to depart. It was dark by now, so we prepared for a night landing on the yacht's helipad. On our training sorties with the *Al Said* we always had the yacht under way, making 5 knots into wind, perfect for us to operate as safely as possible. Sod's law, of course, meant that this time she was at anchor, with wind astern, which made for a tricky approach and landing. I think my adrenaline levels must have helped, as it all went off smoothly. A nice 'Thank you' from HM as he poked his head into the cockpit before he left. Duncan and Saud were outside, by the steps, to salute him as he left.

When I had arrived in Oman, Kevin Smith, another ex-RAF helicopter pilot, was just about to be promoted to Commander of the Royal Flight. Due to some political shenanigans in the Royal Court, he was removed from that position in 1990 and replaced by a serving RAF Air Commodore. Rather than leave Oman, Kevin opted to rejoin the helicopter section as

Oman

Underslung load beneath an SA330J Puma.

a working pilot, which was great for us but a big loss for Royal Flight! That year saw John Nowell get the sack and we gained Tony Wickes from British Airways Helicopters. Tony was ex-RAF (of course) and moved into the training office. He was a breath of fresh air, great sense of humour and definitely a 'glass half full' bloke.

We worked hand in glove with the Royal Oman Police (ROP) when escorting HM and on convoy. Again, they were mainly ex-British military. My good pal Frank Pole had joined them from the North Sea. There were two Omani pilots, Najeeb and Omar, who were the vanguard for future Omanisation of the operation, and an American, Randy Mains, was with them. Randy was a Vietnam Vet who had had an interesting and varied career in flying. Lots of great tales and a passion for safety which he continues to this day, being a prominent advocate for safety in North America. I had the pleasure of flying

Hosni Mubarak and Yasser Arafat to visit HM at his campsite in October.

On the evening of 28 November there was a two-ship task to escort HM on a road trip from Jalali Palace to Bait Al Barka. Jim and Moosa would depart first in AX as General Harcort wanted to have discussions with Jim on arrival. Saad and I were to follow fifteen minutes later in AG. Jim taxied out as I was starting my walk round. I remember hearing a loud noise and looked towards the taxiway. AX had crashed to the ground and was lying on its right side. Spilled fuel was starting to burn. Saad and I started running towards the wreckage, meanwhile Toddy had grabbed a Land Rover and was hurtling towards it. The fire had really taken hold but, as we ran, we saw a figure climb out the top and jump to the ground just as the fire wagons and Toddy got there. Toddy grabbed the figure, threw him in the vehicle and drove off to the Armed Forces Hospital, even before Saad and I got close! The airport Fire Service were busy now, extinguishing the wreckage.

We headed back to the hangar. About half an hour later the Deputy Commander, Mohammed Hamdan, came across and asked me if I would continue with the task, fly to Jalali and meet the General, before covering the road escort. I checked with Saad that he was OK, and he agreed. We had not had any confirmation of casualties at this stage, and I was glad to be getting back in the saddle after the event. General Harcort had questions when we arrived, of course, but there was nothing I could tell him. We continued with the task, flying into the night. When we were finished and back at the airport, we learned the terrible news that Moosa had burned in the wreckage, but Jim had managed to get out, badly burned. Pilots and wives were meeting at Kevin's for a few drinks, so we went there. Unfortunately, Toddy had been badly affected by events and he had had a skin full. He grabbed me, took me aside and asked what the hell I was doing, getting airborne after what had happened? I had to tell him that just because one aircraft crashes, you don't immediately ground the whole fleet!

The crash investigation showed that, once in the hover, the tail rotor pitch mechanism had initiated full maximum pitch. Now, all pilots train for loss of tail rotor or tail driveshaft failure, but to experience full pitch is unthinkable. AX started to spin, but not the way Jim would have expected. Even so, he managed to shut down both engines and they hit the ground spinning, then falling on its right side. Jim was now at the bottom and the only way out was through Moosa's left hand cockpit door. Jim unstrapped as the airframe started to burn. Moosa was now hanging in his straps and couldn't undo them, even with Jim's help. The fire escalated quickly, and Jim realised that if he stayed, he would die. The only escape was to climb over Moosa and out of the top door. He stayed to the last second, receiving serious burns, but unable to release Moosa. Jim was in hospital for a long time and didn't return to flying.

Up Gently

In 1991, Duncan took over as Chief Pilot and Kevin was his deputy. A new arrival in January was a stretched fuselage 332L, similar to North Sea types but extremely dissimilar inside! A very plush and luxurious cabin. The only problem with having a larger helicopter was that we were operating in one of the hottest countries in the world and, at high weights, the performance was not great, an engine failure could prove interesting! There were graphs to calculate maximum weights etc and procedures to follow involving airspeed and heights, which we practised meticulously in the simulator. But Toddy gave me good advice in that, when things go wrong it will happen suddenly and take you by surprise. There will be warning lights illuminating and gauges showing strange information. Prioritise. Rotor rpm will keep you alive. Pull collective until the rpm just starts to decay (droop). You now have the maximum power available. If you are just taking off, decide if that power is enough to trickle forward, easing airspeed up towards VY (remember that?), or, if not, look for an immediate landing spot where you can cushion the impact with maximum collective, losing your rpm as you do, but it doesn't matter then as you are back on Mother Earth. Toddy's take-off brief to his co-pilot was always 'Engine failure, call rotor rpm'. We would try all sorts of weights and weather combinations in the simulator and found that we could fly away at weights above the flight manual limits. So my philosophy for any twin-engined helicopter with an engine failure on take-off is pull to the droop and look for translational lift. If you can't attain it, pick your spot, and cushion the landing. Kiss!

Other arrivals that year were a Crewmen Leader, Baz Hall, an ex-Royal Navy Aircrewman that Duncan wanted to get a grip of the crew training (which he did!), and my old mate from Bond Helicopters, Pete Hogston. I was especially delighted to have Pete join us as we were closer in age than the others and were definitely on the same wavelength. The most important arrival that year was my second daughter, born at the new Muscat University Hospital!

The routine of convoys and deployments to Salalah continued, interspersed with VIP tasks. HM was camping in the interior in February 1992 when General Harcort arranged a demonstration of Royal Guard firepower. A dais was built facing a large area where various weapons would be discharged. For one part of the demonstration two Pumas, flown by Nick and me, would skirt past each side of the dais at zero feet, quick stop into wind facing HM, discharge 16 troops each before lifting and departing behind the dais. Great fun. It started well and looked good, perfectly timed as we slowed for landing, kicking up sand and creating a 'Brown Out', which was normal and something we dealt with on a daily basis. At this point I must mention that there was a quirk with the 330 Puma, well known by pilots who flew it, in that when the engines dropped to idle, they were slow to accelerate. So, here I am, on the ground with troops leaving the cab. I call 'Ready' when they've gone and wait for Nick's

'Ready' to coordinate our take-off. 'Lifting' and I foolishly pull up maximum collective. The rotors bite hard, kicking up dust, but starting to slow down, waiting for the engines to spool up! I've now created a huge dust cloud. As the engines wind up and the rotors wind down, they suddenly meet and I lift quickly, spinning inside my self-made cloud. It must have looked impressive as I popped out at about 100 feet, stopped the spin and dived away! Lesson learned.

That same month Phil Stevens, Saud and I flew the Minister of Finance to Duqm, where an ancient Omani chap came aboard, swinging his goat-herding stick and was shown into the cockpit jump seat by Saud. He was to direct us where to go to meet with senior families of the Bedouin tribes in the Harrasis desert, where the minister was to distribute largesse from HM. Now we didn't have GPS in those days, but we had something better. Goat Poking Stick. We got airborne and this chap directed us with his stick along dry wadis, towards slight hillocks and turning at isolated trees, flying for about half an hour until the classic desert oasis appeared on the nose, a few palm trees with a pond in the middle and Bedouin tents erected around the outside. We shut down close by and the Bedouin leaders hustled the minister into a tent. The rest of us sat down around a large mat placed on the ground under the trees where we were offered coffee and dates, as was the custom and not to be refused!

Eventually the minister reappeared and joined

us at the mat where the head man sat down next to me. A large dish of aromatic rice and Goat meat was placed centrally for all to share, two cooked Goat skulls poking from the rice. The minister led off and we all joined in. The head man grabbed a skull, and the minister told me that I would be honoured with a delicacy. I saw that the eyeballs were still there and was dreading what might happen. However, he cracked open the jaw and sliced out the tongue, placing it in front of me with a smile on his face. He knew exactly what I had been thinking and he and the minister had a good laugh! The tongue was delicious. The rice dish was cleared away and a plate of apples and oranges were placed there. An incredible luxury for nomadic tribesmen. We declined the fruit and the minister stood up, ready to leave. As we walked to the helicopter, children appeared from the tents and fell upon the fruit. A big treat for them and there were smiles and waving as we lifted to depart back to the convoy site, now using our Loran navigation equipment!

It was a great time. Oman was a beautiful place to live, the job was fantastic and paying top money and I couldn't have been happier. That year saw another cruise around the Mediterranean in the summer and then back to Salalah for the Khareef. Happy days.

1993 began with a 'Meet the People' convoy on the road to Salalah, where HM only stayed for a couple of weeks before flying north. He returned to Salalah in June, and we deployed the helicopters there for the summer. My world was about to implode.

Up Gently

I flew a training trip on a Thursday in early July and was rostered a day off the next day, Friday, so decided to have a beer or two at the Oryx bar at the nearby Sergeants Mess in the Army camp across the main road from our gated accommodation. It was about one kilometre, an easy walk but I decided to drive. You can see what's coming! After a relaxing evening involving more than a few beers I got into my Toyota Corolla provided by Royal Flight and started the journey home. I woke up sitting in the car, on top of the roundabout outside our accommodation compound. I had hit some large boulders placed there and the front end was stoved in. The guards came running and dragged me out, taking me to the gatehouse, where I was able to telephone Pete, who came to collect me, take me to his bungalow and started pouring coffee into me. Meanwhile, the police had arrived on scene and were insisting that I be brought to the guardhouse. Pete had alerted Duncan to the situation, and he was arguing with the police, close to being arrested himself! But Pete had cleaned me up, although my forehead was a mess where I had hit the windscreen, and he took me to the police, who allowed him to take me to the hospital. They treated me there and a blood alcohol sample was taken. I can never thank Pete enough for taking care of me that night. I had been a complete idiot and could have killed myself or, worse, killed someone else.

The Senior Royal Flight officer in Salalah was Abdullah Ateeq. He was a gentleman and a good friend. It so happened that his brother-in-law was Chief of police there. Abdullah took me to his office the next day and, after the usual Arab greetings and pleasantries (which took about twenty minutes), Abdullah broached the question of the blood sample and possible charges. 'What blood sample? I don't believe there is one!' And so my possible conviction disappeared. Abdullah saved my neck that day, I was luckier than a couple of our engineers who had both done jail time in the past for drink-driving. The commander of Royal Flight was not so forgiving, of course, my behaviour was completely unacceptable and so my contract was terminated.

In life I had always made decisions knowing that if they were the wrong ones then regrets were of no use, decision made so get on with it, good or bad. But the decision to drive that night is the only one I do regret.

Chapter 7

Firefighting

Back in UK and looking for a job! The North Sea companies weren't hiring, and I didn't have any contacts in the smaller companies. However, before I left Oman, Tony Wickes had been in touch with his old employer in Aberdeen, British International Helicopters, and written some nice things about me, knowing that I was sending a CV off to them. As it turned out, they were looking for an experienced Super Puma pilot who was current in underslung load operations, to be employed on a freelance basis for a couple of months. They were part of Canadian Helicopters Corporation, who had won a contract to provide firefighting Helicopters to the Greek government. I received a phone call from their Chief Pilot, who wanted me to travel to Aberdeen immediately to renew my UK Instrument rating and discuss the operation. I was up there like a shot. Everyone there knew who I was and where I had come from. Lots of head shaking and disbelief that I could have lost a plum job in such a fashion. I could only agree.

Firefighting

I was straight into my flying test, which went well, then introduced to my fellow pilot on the contract, Ron Managh, a New Zealander who was employed on the North Sea but had cut his teeth on bush flying and had the correct mindset for what we were to do in Greece. It wasn't a job for bus drivers going rig to rig!

I headed back home for a couple of days to pack and get ready. Ron flew the aircraft down to Cardiff for a refuel, along with Stu Mould, an ex-RAF bloke who was the company test pilot. The three of us then completed the transit to Athens, overnighting en route in Bordeaux and Naples. Ron and Stu were glad to see me as the aircraft was not to North Sea specification and had Loran navigation equipment, the same fit that was in the Oman aircraft. I was able to programme the route very quickly and give the blokes instruction in using it. When we arrived in Athens it was a hive of activity. Helicopters were arriving daily, some from North America in Antonov freighters to be assembled there, some (like us), being flown in direct. There was a mix of types, Super Pumas, Sikorskys and Hueys. We were allocated our firefighting equipment, a huge 'Bambi' bucket which held four tons of water and a 100-foot-long cable to suspend it from. There was an electrical connection to be plugged in at the bucket end and at the aircraft's hook. A large bubble window was fitted to the left side cockpit door to enable the pilot on that side to hang over the collective lever and see the bucket below, with a button on the collective to release the water when required. We set about training in the use of it, Stu was there to write up the Standard Operating Procedures and the regulatory requirements for the Civil Aviation Authority. I was surprised how easily I took to flying while bent double to the left while looking straight down! We determined that the right-hand pilot would fly the run-in to the fire, handing control to the left seat pilot for the final few yards and the release of the water on target. The same procedure for picking up water, right seat flying to the dunking point over the sea, left seat dunking and picking the full bucket out of the water, with the right seat calling the power being used.

After a couple of days, we were sent off to the island of Samos to begin operations. We had a nasty scare as we left Athens. The tower cleared us to cross the runway approach after a landing 757. As we crossed the centreline it felt as though a massive hand had grabbed the fuselage and shaken us violently. I thought the main gearbox was detaching! It was purely wake turbulence from the landing Boeing, being low and slow with full flap it created a vicious vortex behind, which we were too close to. Another lesson learned and I gave landing fixed-wing a wide berth from then on.

Arriving at Samos we could see the destruction wreaked by the wildfires they had suffered. It seemed like half of the island was charred and blackened. We were only there for one week before being re-tasked to Rhodes. We were stationed at a disused military airfield called

Firefighting

On standby with British International Helicopters.

Maritsa, inland from the main civil airport. Co-located with us was another Super Puma, marked with decals of 'Ontario Hydro Board', and crewed by Canadians. There was a barrack room by the hangar, where Greek firefighters were billeted, sixteen of them, eight to each helicopter. We kept the Bambi bucket and cable stowed in the cabin and, when called, the firefighters would leap on board, we would head off and pick a suitable drop-off point for them to start beating and building firebreaks. We would then get the bucket and cable out, attach them, then head off to the closest beach to pick up water and begin dousing the fire. It worked very smoothly, and we had some good results. I remember one farmer jumping up and down, clapping his hands, as we extinguished a blaze threatening his property. It was enjoyable flying and very worthwhile.

Up Gently

This was classed as 'Aerial Work' and so there were no crew duty restrictions. We were available from dawn to dusk, seven days a week. Evenings were spent in the tourist bars and, my God, those Canadians could drink! My Kiwi friend and I felt duty bound to keep them company and, despite my recent chequered history, it was a work hard/ play hard environment.

All good things come to an end, and late in October we left Rhodes for Athens, meeting up with the other crews who had been deployed all over Greece. Many of them had been much busier than us, especially on the mainland North of Athens. One night there and we returned to England with just one overnight stop in Ajaccio in Corfu. Our final destination was Beccles heliport in East Anglia, a British International base. Now I was looking for employment again. Still no joy on the North Sea and nothing overland. I popped up to Norwich Airport to meet with Gerry Hermer, a former RAF SAR Pilot who had a firm called Sterling Helicopters. A friend from 72 Sqn days was there, Dick Bendy, but Gerry had no work for me either. Possibilities for the future, but nothing immediately. It was to be the first (and only) time I was unemployed at Christmas!

Chapter 8

Police

Devon and Cornwall

January 1994 and my barrage of CVs to every helicopter company paid off. Aeromega had the contract to supply pilots to Devon and Cornwall Constabulary, to fly their Bolkow BO105 from police HQ at Middlemoor, Exeter. One pilot was leaving, and they needed someone at short notice, to see out the 6 months remaining on the contract. I was living just north of Exmoor, on the outskirts of Minehead, about a fifty-minute commute to Exeter. The unit manager was Capt. Paul Hannant who had been with SOAF in Salalah in 1988. I was asked to attend an interview, which went well on both sides, and began converting to the Bolkow in February. My instructor was Nick Holbrook, an affable older guy and a very good pilot. I hated the Bolkow at first, it was tiny and cramped. I had only flown larger helicopters up to now and I didn't get into the Bolkow so much as put it on! Tiny little pedals, tiny little throttle levers in the cockpit roof and a feeling of being squeezed in. But it soon endeared itself to me.

Possibly the smallest twin engined helicopter going, with two of the engines which powered the ubiquitous Bell Jetranger, making it powerful for its size and safe. Its rotor head was made from titanium and was rigid, with no drag or flapping hinges for the blades. This made it very responsive but twitchy and unforgiving. Not an easy helicopter to fly but once you had the feel of it, there was none better. In that respect it was like a powerful sports car. Not something suitable to learn to drive in but, for an experienced motorist, a challenge and delight. It was fully aerobatic, but the CAA forbid extreme manoeuvres. It had one nasty vice. If you got yourself into a descending right-hand turn with high power (raised collective) it would 'settle' into that condition, and you could find yourself with full left pedal and full left cyclic but still turning and descending! The only way out was to lower the collective (increasing your rate of descent!) which would give more authority to the left corrections. If you were close to the ground, you were going to crash. It even caught out Bolkow's test pilot, Sigi Hoffman, who died giving a display.

Landing back at base was interesting to begin with. There was a trolley, not much bigger than the skids, which was used to take the helicopter in and out of the hangar. There was a U-shaped mark on the front right corner which was the marker to place the front of the skid. You had to be very precise, which wasn't easy in such a twitchy machine! If the collective was to be lowered with a skid not quite in place, you ran the risk of it slipping off the trolley and possibly leading to a dynamic rollover, which is as dramatic as it sounds and not to be experienced. I found it intimidating for the first few landings and, regardless of how well I'd flown, I knew the final challenge was always waiting!

I started on shift in late February and really enjoyed the unpredictable nature of every task which came to us. You had to think on your feet quickly and prioritise what was needed. The experienced police sergeants on board had the use of a high-powered day/night video camera mounted in a pod, and a powerful Nightsun searchlight. This was before the days when every police helicopter has a television crew on board, so it was all very new and exciting. I looked forward to every shift!

On the second of March I had the enjoyable task of flying the Chief Constable and Her Majesty's Inspector of Constabulary from police HQ to the Scilly Isles, refuelling at Penzance heliport outbound and inbound. It was the annual inspection of the force and the inspector wanted to visit the sergeant and couple of constables based on the islands. It was barely legal for us to do the trip, we could fly ten minutes from land without emergency floats, so from coasting out at Land's End, to coasting in at the first rock of the Scillies, it had to be no more than twenty minutes. Which it was of course. I was taken aback at how gorgeous the islands were, with beautiful beaches. Not much crime!

I enjoyed flying around spectacular Devon and Cornwall for the next few months, knowing it would come to an end in mid-July. There were a few stolen car chases, missing person searches, all the usual police work, plus casualty evacuations in Devon as it was in the days before their Air Ambulance was running. At the end of June, I again had the pleasure of flying the Chief Constable, this time to the island of Lundy. On the way, we landed on the lawn in front of Castle Hill, the country house of Lady Arun, who was the Deputy Lieutenant of Devon, to take her on board for the short hop across the Bristol Channel to visit Lundy. We put down in a field next to the visitor centre, but I had to spend my time shooing off inquisitive cattle who were threatening to damage the helicopter, while the VIP passengers enjoyed a look around and tea and cakes. I was glad when they returned and we headed back to Exeter, dropping Lady Arun at her residence on the way.

All good things come to an end, and so it was with my time in Devon and Cornwall. Police Aviation Services (PAS) were taking on the contract and I spent the last few shifts there line training one incoming pilot, Pete Ashby, who was also ex-RAF. Paul Hannant had lobbied hard with PAS to take me on, which they did, although not in Devon and Cornwall. I was about to move again.

Police

Sussex

Normally, pilots joining PAS were started as 'Floaters', filling in on units all around the country for pilots on leave or sick etc., so I was lucky to be offered a permanent position with Sussex. The unit was based at Shoreham airfield on the south coast, a picturesque setting mainly used for private flying. I was commuting there from Minehead to begin with until I could sell my house and bring the family. I was staying in the Police Section House at Worthing and it was a great way to meet the local Bobbies and settle in to the job. I was replacing Dave Russell who was moving to PAS HQ at Staverton airfield, as the new Chief Pilot. There were two other pilots on the unit, Dave Williams (ex-Army Air Corps)

Flying the Sussex Police Bolkow 105 based at Shoreham (first left, second row).

and Chief Pilot Ian Brown (ex-Royal Navy). The helicopter was also a Bolkow 105 (on a trolley!) and the crew comprised one pilot, one police observer and one paramedic, as it was also the Sussex Air Ambulance and about a quarter of the work was Medical. There were only two such units in the country, Sussex and Wiltshire, where paramedics were carried routinely, and as such, it was really a joint Police/Ambulance operation. It worked very well, paramedics helping with the police tasks, and pilots and police acting as aides to the paramedic. It was the best of both worlds, and the flying was fantastic and varied. Shifts were either daytime, or evening, running in to midnight. We would extend if need be for late tasks, and we were also on call at home if required through the night.

Landing for medical emergencies at night was probably the most dangerous flying I was called on to do. A suitable location would be picked out using the FLIR camera, then it would be illuminated with the Nightsun searchlight. After identifying possible hazards an approach would be made, preferably steep, down the Nightsun beam, all eyes on board scanning for wires and obstructions. At about fifty feet the Nightsun had to be extinguished as it could ignite dry grass or other materials if it came too close! The final landing was made using the standard landing lamp. Great sighs of relief when safely down and the paramedic could dash off to the scene.

I was caught out once by a dangerous aerodynamic condition called 'Vortex Ring'. In the hover you are using a lot of power pushing air down through the rotors. If you begin to descend then the air coming up meets the air being pushed down and they effectively cancel each other out. So you lose all of your lift and you are going down! Perversely, if you raise your collective lever, it makes things worse by increasing the vortex. The only recovery is to get out of that 'Ring' by lowering the Collective and using cyclic to tilt the disc, moving into clean air, then raising the collective when you have airspeed. You can lose a lot of height doing this. I was in the hover at about 1,000 feet above a road accident at night with the Nightsun illuminating the scene, looking for a safe landing site using the FLIR. This task was for the police officer in the left seat, as they had the screen in front of them, but the temptation was always there to peek over and have a look. It was while I was doing this that we started to descend. Slowly, imperceptibly at first, but building up. It was just the hairs on the back of my neck warned me, but I looked inside, saw the vertical speed indicator showing 800 feet per minute descent, so dropped the collective and shoved the nose hard forward, causing some alarm to my colleagues on board! Our descent increased of course before the airspeed indicator registered and I pulled full power on the collective to climb away. I reckon we pulled up about 200 ft above ground level. A close thing.

Jobs were always varied and interesting. It was fun, when returning at night, to spot the glowing roofs of houses with marijuana growing in the loft. Just note the address and they would get a knock from their local Bobby.

For an assist to the customs force, we landed with lights out at a pre-selected site near Beachy Head, before getting airborne to illuminate a large yacht in Eastbourne Bay, which was returning from South America. They were boarded as soon as our Nightsun lit them up, a large quantity of drugs being found on board.

In August of '95 we picked up a diver who had been brought ashore near Newhaven, suffering from the bends. This meant an extreme low-level transit along the coast to Lee-on-Solent where we transferred him to the Coastguard helicopter for onward travel to a hyperbaric chamber.

In September we rushed to a house North of Chichester where a 2-year-old child had fallen into a garden pond at her grandparents' house and was not responding. I kept the rotors running as the paramedic, John Hopkin and Inspector Chris Poole, the unit boss, rushed into the house to collect her. They then came back on board, John taking her with him on the back seat to treat her. It was only ten minutes to the hospital but after five minutes or so John had her responding, then crying loudly! I looked over at Chris and we both smiled with relief. I was to learn that her survival was due to the 'Mammalian Dive Reflex', where the body shuts down when immersed, to conserve oxygen. It is a natural phenomenon, especially in young children. It was to play a part in another job a few years down the line.

Police

In '95 two Constables joined the unit, Nigel Tinkler and Juley (spelt EY not IE!) Hickman, both had completed extensive training, and both were bloody good operators. I had the pleasure of flying with Juley on her first operational shift. She tracked and found four suspects who were hiding in a rural area at night after a burglary. It was a great bit of work, but I think she was disappointed after that, that she didn't get the same excitement on every shift!

I was flying with Nigel when we had a report of a stolen vehicle heading to Newhaven. We spotted it in the town, and they made off at speed towards Eastbourne. It was daylight and as they left the built-up area Nigel thought we should 'Show Out' to them, coming down low so they know they are being followed and have no chance of escape. There was a large open field alongside the road, so I flew low alongside them, putting them on Nigel's side. They were doing about 80 mph, and we were low, and close. There were four lads in the car and Nigel was grinning at them, giving them a thumbs up. They didn't slow down but as I gained height again, they crashed on a bend as a traffic car arrived. No injuries but four in custody. How we laughed!

Chris Poole's deputy was an old-school sergeant called John Tickner. He was a straight-talking bloke who would reminisce about the good old days when coppers could dispense some instant justice occasionally. As the force was moving into a multicultural, diverse world, all coppers had to attend a day's 'Community

Awareness Training' (CAT), to change their attitude towards minorities. I was on shift with John the day after he had been there. I asked him if he had found it interesting. 'Yes', he said. 'But you are still a fat Geordie bastard!' Love him.

When Chris was posted to another job he passed the reins to Inspector Cliff Gale, a big bloke—a gentle bear of a man—who was still playing rugby in his forties! When Cliff and I were crewed together on a night shift, the weight of the two of us in the front seats, plus the big Nightsun searchlight bolted onto the nose, meant that the Centre of Gravity exceeded the forward limit! If I had lifted into the hover, the cyclic stick would have had restricted authority when pulling it backwards, leading to possible control problems. The solution was to place a full Jerry can of water as far back as possible in the rear hold. Or not to fly with Cliff!

Kent Police didn't have their own helicopter so they would call on us if we were available. In January of '97 they made such a request to assist in the search for a vulnerable missing person. It was after dark, and the forecast was for possible snow showers, but they were expected to be north of us in Surrey and up to London. As we set off, all was well but we hadn't found any trace of the misper before reaching the fuel minimum to head back to Shoreham. We left Kent, heading west and then the snow started falling. I was not too perturbed as I knew it was to the north of us and we were probably getting stuff from the edge of it. But then it thickened, and we descended to about 500 feet above ground. We were North of Hastings with high ground between us and the sea and there were big high-tension wires in the vicinity. The visibility reduced dramatically in the snow, and I was considering turning around but not knowing how bad it was behind us either. It was pitch black by now, save one source of light on the ground, a pub with a floodlit car Park! That was it, a quick jink into wind and lined up to land there. Plenty of spaces. The landing lamp just made things worse as it only illuminated the falling snow! Just using the car park lights we made it down safely. It was blowing a blizzard now. I shut down the engines and we decamped into the pub to the amazement of the landlord and his guests! Headquarters sent transport to collect us and drive us back to Shoreham and some poor copper was detailed off to guard the helicopter overnight. The pub was the Rainbow Trout at Broad Oak, and the landlord treated us to a meal and a drink, on the house, before we departed. There would be no further flying that night! I returned to the pub on a private visit a few weeks later, to thank the landlord and present him with a framed aerial photo of the pub.

I was on a cliff top search near Peacehaven one day with John Tickner and paramedic Simon Stevens. John was using the gyro-stabilised binoculars as we gently flew parallel to the cliff, just offshore. Suddenly there was a smell of burning and smoke appeared. The power lead to the binoculars was on fire! Smoke quickly started to fill the cabin as John threw the binoculars into the back, straight on to Simon's lap. He then dumped them to the floor as I switched off both generators and set up to land. The smoke was thick now, both sliding doors were opened in the rear, and I was looking through a small sliding panel in my door. I landed on, John and Simon immediately fully opened the doors and exited, coughing and hacking like fury. I stopped the engines, rotor brake on and joined the blokes outside. Despite the assault on their lungs, they had both lit cigarettes and were puffing away furiously! It turned out that there was no circuit breaker to the power lead, and it had overheated.

Shoreham Airfield hosted an air display once a year in September and we always participated. I was delighted to be asked to be the display pilot, my spirited handling had obviously been noted, plus my previous incarnation as Wessex display pilot was handy. The Bolkow was fully aerobatic, but we had constraints with the equipment fitted. It was still possible to give a good account of its capabilities, but I worked up slowly, learning its limitations and my limitations. It's difficult to impart the absolute joy I got from throwing that machine around the sky. It reacted so quickly to control inputs due to the rigid rotor head, it was more like an extension of your limbs than a piece of equipment. Eventually, I was ready, and our Flight Operations inspector from the Civil Aviation Authority visited to give his approval (or not!). All went well and I was cleared to show off in front of a big crowd again!

I attended a reunion of RAF Support

Helicopters at the RAF Benson Officers Mess and met up with a lot of old friends. A great amount of alcohol was consumed that evening, but I was proud to say that the last blokes standing at the bar, at the end of the night, were the three PAS pilots, myself, Pete Ashby, and Graham Budden, chief pilot for Kent Air Ambulance. Graham and two paramedics died on 26 July 1998 in a crash where the helicopter hit low-level power lines when returning to base. Dave Williams then moved across to Kent and we received a new pilot in Sussex, Pete Rowlinson, a graduate of the Empire Test Pilots school and a brain the size of a planet as well as being a very nice bloke!

As Police flying was carried out using Visual Flight Rules (VFR) I was not able to keep my instrument rating current and, after five years since my Greece trip, it was due to expire in August 1998. As far as I knew, none of PAS's pilots held an instrument rating but the company saw the benefit of keeping mine current. PAS arranged for me to travel to Devon for some brush-up training and test ride from Exeter with my old Bond mentor, Dick Metson. Unfortunately, when I arrived Dick had caught a bug and couldn't fly. Before heading back, I thought I would pop in and see old friends at the Police unit. As it turned out, Paul Hannant was still the boss there and he had recently qualified as an instrument rating Examiner. He was happy to go flying with me in their Bolkow, which was now their spare aircraft, having upgraded to a Bolkow 117. The idea was to make an assessment, see what training I would need and make further flights. As it turned out, the flight went perfectly, and he was happy to renew my rating there and then! I was over the moon. My hours on Microsoft Flight Simulator, at home, going over and over the procedures, had paid off.

Into 1999 and excitement on the unit about our upgrade to the McDonnell Douglas MD902 Explorer, which was due in the spring. Ian Brown and Cliff Gale had been researching which type would be best suited to the Sussex operation and getting a proper perspective on some of the bullshit payload and performance figures pushed out by the manufacturers. The Explorer fitted the bill nicely. It had a large cabin with sliding doors on both sides, excellent for carrying patients and lots of room for the paramedic and equipment. The cockpit was up to date with video instrumentation and a delightful feature called 'Display by Exception', where temperatures and pressures were invisible unless they approached a limit. I was never happy with this, I like to see gauges and moving needles! The cyclic stick was unusual with an up and over design which worked very well. The whole cockpit had been designed by pilots, apparently, not engineers, and it showed. The engines were of the Full Authority Digital Engine Control (FADEC) type but with manual throttles on the collective if required. A semi-rigid rotor head, similar to the Apache (so I'm told) but the biggest missing feature was the tail rotor. No tail rotor (NOTAR)! There was a tail boom, much like a tube, which had two slots

The McDonnell Douglas MD902 Explorer.

running along its length. A fan blew air down the tube, 70% of which exited through those slots. This air, combined with the rotor downwash, produced a sideways couple which counteracted the torque on the main rotor. The remaining 30% went to a movable duct at the rear of the boom, controlled by the pilot's pedals, which provided directional control. Once you started moving forward two large vertical fins kept you pointing straight. They were not attached to any flight controls but were completely automatic: the Vertical Stabilisation Control System (VSCS). Yet another acronym to learn! The machine was powerful and safe. I have to say that, of all the types I flew, the Explorer was definitely my favourite.

1999 brought personal problems to the fore. I haven't talked about my personal life much as

Up Gently

I want to keep my rambling confined to flying but things happened which affected my ability to be as professional as possible. Wife number one had decided that she wanted away. She had qualified as a paramedic and was working for the Ambulance service. She told me that she wanted nothing to do with her daughters and she would keep all her wages, contributing nothing towards their upkeep. I divorced her for 'Effective Abandonment', leaving me as a single Dad to my daughters who were 6 and 9. Their mother had minimum contact with them for the first year. I was able to work my shifts by employing fantastic au-pair girls from the Czech Republic and France. It was stressful practically, emotionally, and financially. I remember one day, in the car, my 6-year-old saying 'Daddy, I'm jealous of you'. I said, 'You don't have to be jealous darling! Why are you saying that'? She replied 'Well, when you were a little boy, you saw your mummy every day'! I felt like someone had grabbed my heart and was squeezing it. My emotional state was not good, and it showed in my next check ride. I barely reached the standard required and I think I was becoming a liability. It all came to a head one night in October. I had been out for a long walk from home, trying to clear my head. When I returned Cliff was at the house and ready for a cup of tea and a long chat. He recognised that I was under a great deal of stress and could not have been more sympathetic or understanding. He told me that I would be having appointments with the force psychologist and would be

Police

Aerobatics in the Explorer.

grounded for a while. He had arranged with PAS
to have a replacement pilot in the meantime.
Looking back, it was the best thing to do, but at
the time, I was devastated. That's when future
wife number two, Debbie, moved in and sorted
me out. Without her intervention I don't know if
I could have returned to flying. But I did, after a
month or so, and never looked back. I had never
understood the concepts of anxiety or stress,
always thinking 'Pull your socks up and get on
with it', but Cliff was a fantastic boss and knew
the illness and the remedy.

Back to flying and on 19 December we attended
a nasty road accident where a driver had tried
a dodgy overtake and hit another car head-on.
An older gentleman, he was in a bad way, but
the paramedics did their usual fantastic job

and loaded him into the helicopter, still alive. It was a short flight to Eastbourne hospital where he was rushed into A&E but, unfortunately, he was too badly injured and passed away. When his wallet was found it was discovered that he was Desmond Llewellyn, 'Q' from the first Bond movies. A sad end.

The new millennium began, and we were enjoying the capabilities of the Explorer immensely. We had been using the PAS spare machine until the Sussex one was completed, it was delivered on the 15th of February. On the 19th of February I was on shift with Sgt Paul Furnell, paramedic Mike Crockford, and we had the pleasure of the company of Dr Priscilla Noble-Mathews, an amazing lady who, as part of the Sussex Immediate Care Scheme (SIMCAS), would attend serious accidents and give her time and expertise to us on her days off from her surgery. She also always turned up with a cake she had baked! It was about lunchtime when we received a call from force HQ to say that a four-year-old child had slipped on rocks at Shoreham beach and had been carried out to sea, about 100 yards offshore. We were airborne immediately and were overhead about 12 minutes after she had fallen into the water. She was floating, lifeless, and we could see her mother running up and down the beach frantically. One gentleman appeared to be stripping off, ready to dive in towards her daughter. Before continuing, I have to say that in the previous November, Mike and I had seen a young boy drown after being swept off the undercliff walk east of Brighton Marina. It was a very rough sea, but Mike had volunteered then to wear a lifejacket and jump in with a spare for the boy. I said no, it was far too rough, and we would have ended up with two casualties! I'm sure that was in both of our minds as we looked at the girl.

Shoreham inshore lifeboat was being manned up with its volunteer crew being called in but would take at least another fifteen minutes to get here. The Coastguard helicopter from Lee-On-Solent, winch equipped, would be at least twenty minutes. We couldn't let her die. There was only a slight swell, and the wind was blowing offshore. Mike volunteered to step out onto the skid wearing a life jacket and connected by the monkey harness, in order to grab her. I had no hesitation in agreeing. I began descending towards her little body, I could see that she was wearing a furry coat and still not moving. Cabin door open, Mike stepped out and moved forward to be next to me, making it easier to get close to her. I was breathing heavily; I could hear it over the intercom. Paul said 'Careful, careful' as the skids touched the water. I appreciated his concern!

We were kicking up a lot of spray and while being into wind, the swell was coming from behind and from a situation where the skids were just touching the water, suddenly they were below the surface and Mike was up to his knees! I was seriously concerned about the proximity of the Notar to the sea, but we were committed now. Any mishandling, any engine cough, would see us ditching in the water. We were close to her now. Mike said, 'Right a bit more' and we were next to her. With one hand on the door handle, he used the other to grab her coat and pulled her up under his armpit. 'Got her!' he exclaimed. I squeezed up the collective and moved forward to the beach while Mike came inboard so that he and Dr Priscilla could work on the girl. As we touched the beach there was a shout of, 'She's alive!' They had resuscitated her, and I just gave a silent thanks as the doctor said that she needed to get to hospital quickly.

The mother was with a police officer on the beach and running towards us, but there was no time to get her onboard and we set off straightaway. Worthing hospital was less than five minutes away and there was a new helipad area cleared in the car park next to the front entrance. The officer on the beach brought the mother by road. As soon as we landed, Mike and Priscilla were out of the door carrying the girl into A&E. Later that day she was transferred by road ambulance up to St George's hospital in London for further treatment.

When we got back to base, I rang Cliff and told him what had happened and that we might expect some press interest. Which turned out to be an understatement! It became a major story, and every national newspaper printed it. The whole thing had been caught on a CCTV camera further along the seafront, so BBC and ITV news showed it nationally. We were in constant demand for interviews and comments. Definitely having our fifteen minutes of fame! Thankfully the girl made a full recovery and she and her dad came to visit us a few weeks later with TV news cameras in tow! What had saved her was the Mammalian Dive Reflex mentioned earlier. We all received Royal Humane Society awards, which was nice. The unit also received special attention from the Civil Aviation Authority, the chief Flight Operations Inspector visiting, along with our local bloke, to discuss what had happened and to let us know that they were concerned. But they knew, and we knew, that given that situation, any police pilot would have done the same thing. I certainly did not want to contemplate ever doing it again!

My colleague from my time on 72 Sqn, Norman Lees, would fly into Shoreham occasionally. He

'We all received Royal Humane Society Awards.'

had made a name for himself in the aviation world and was a 747 Captain with Virgin Atlantic. He also flew many different types of restored aircraft and took care of the collection belonging to Dave Gilmour, the guitarist with Pink Floyd, one of which was a P51 Mustang which Norman displayed all over the country. The last time I saw him was when he had just brought Mr. Gilmour's Beech Staggerwing to Shoreham for a service. On the 8th of April Norman was instructing in a two-seat Spitfire at Goodwood airfield which flipped and crashed on short finals. Both occupants were killed.

A very good friend on the unit was PC Steve Cleghorn, an ex-traffic cop and advanced motorcycle instructor. Being a police observer gave him the taste for aviation and he went on to gain his Airline Transport Licence and fly executive jets and airliners. We were on shift one day and received a call to Beachy Head, where a gentleman had been seen to jump. One of the sadder aspects of working in Sussex was that Beachy Head was a favourite suicide spot and we were regularly called on to collect the bodies. On this occasion we couldn't see him. We knew where he had jumped from, so knew where he should have landed, but no trace. Eventually we went to the top of the cliff, knowing where he was last seen, then hovered at the edge, looking down visually and with the infra-red camera. Steve saw him on camera. He had ended up at the bottom sliding behind a piece of rock there. I swung us down to the bottom and landed on, Steve and the paramedic got out with the body bag and went to where he was. Steve described it later: 'He was upright, on his feet but with a surprised look on his face'! Very dead, of course. They pulled him out, bagged him up and we took him to Eastbourne hospital for the mortuary.

While I was at Sussex, TV companies had woken up to the fact that police helicopter operations made for good viewing and we had a lot of requests to ride along with us. Not so easy in the little Bolkow, although we did feature in one episode of *Blues and Twos*, and one of *On Patrol*. The weather on the day of filming *On Patrol* was atrocious, raining solidly. We attended two road accidents and it looks thoroughly grim. Later, with the Explorer, we could more easily carry a cameraman and we featured in two episodes of *Chopper Coppers*. It got to the point where I was being recognised by members of the public when out and about!

My time in Sussex was coming to a close (for now). PAS Chief Pilot, Dave Russell, had tickets for the West Ham v Newcastle football match and invited me along, knowing that Newcastle United was my passion. I should have known that there is no such thing as a free lunch. We were having a chat over a couple of pints before the game, and he asked me if I would consider a move north? He knew I was interested in Northumberland Air Ambulance, but he had a different proposition. The medical arm of PAS, MAS, had bid on the contract for the new Yorkshire Air Ambulance and he wanted to pencil me in as Chief Pilot to get it up and running. I agreed straight away. Newcastle lost but I was on a winner!

Chapter 9

Yorkshire Air Ambulance

I knew how to deal with stress now and it was just as well, because I was about to load myself up with it. Of course, there is good stress and bad. The good was that I married Debbie in August and we uprooted from Sussex with my daughters, moving initially to Harrogate. I was at MAS headquarters at Gloucester Airport in September, meeting the first paramedics from Yorkshire, who were commencing their training there. A wonderful bunch of blokes, all experienced paramedics and as keen as mustard to get started. There was a lot to do before we would be ready! The paramedic manager was Mick Lindley, and he was a driving force in the early days, passionate about what we could achieve and wanting nothing less than perfection in what we did. I received briefings on what I needed to do regarding the CAA requirements for a new operation and was told that I would finish training the paramedics in Yorkshire. This was news to me as I had never been involved in training or examining and had

October 2000
The Pioneers
Back Row: Neil Hemingway, Chris Croden, Paul Gibson, Steve Wilson, Dave Hey, Steve Morrell.
Front Row: Mick Lindley (Unit Manager), John Sutherland (Chief Pilot)

no guidelines to follow! Steve Bidmead, a senior MAS pilot, said to me, 'You've been doing this job for years, you know what's required of them, just pass it on!' I found the whole idea more intimidating than flying heads of state, but just had to get on with it.

The helicopter was a Bolkow and our yellow Yorkshire Air Ambulance would not be ready until shortly before the launch date on 25 October. Before then, we had a spare training BO105 which I delivered to Leeds Airport on 30 September. YAA was being hosted by Multiflight, a training/charter operation on the west side of the airfield and they had provided a portacabin outside their offices. I remember landing, tying down the helicopter, and entering the sparsely furnished cabin carrying the box given to me by MAS, containing headed notepaper, envelopes and ball point pens, red and blue. That was it! I knew that this was the start of something really big, but for now it seemed very daunting.

We began training in the first week of October. Initially I was concentrating on safety in and around the helicopter, once those rotors start turning and the radios are crackling there are many distractions which can cause unforced errors. I made sure that there was no misunderstanding when it came to opening doors and disembarking/embarking, and that they would maintain a safe area around the helicopter. We would be close to members of the public and the paramedics would be responsible for keeping them safe also. On each flight, on the way to an incident, one was in the left-hand cockpit seat, facing forwards and they could act as my co-pilot, tuning radios and navaids, and helping with navigation.

When carrying a patient, the left-hand seat was reversed so that that paramedic could be dealing with medical matters. No satellite navigation in those days, they were taught to use ordinance survey maps and A to Z directories for each town, eventually being able to direct me to a telephone box on a street corner, if need be. It was a difficult skill to master, some

Yorkshire Air Ambulance

The Yorkshire Air Ambulance Bolkow.

were better than others, but the blokes worked hard and all reached a good standard. Lookout was paramount, we would be operating outside controlled airspace mainly, and I wanted all eyes outside as much as possible, especially on approach to landing when electricity and telephone wires can take the edge off your day. Landing site selection was important, knowing where we could land and helping select a good spot close to incidents. The five 'S' words were taught Size, Shape, Slope, Surface, Surround, to which I added a sixth 'Access'. Not exactly an 'S' but it had that sound! It was pointless finding a landing site close to the incident if there was a six-foot barbed wire fence to get over.

In amongst the training was the formidable task of becoming an operational unit on the 25th of October. I had to prepare a local hospital landing site directory for the whole of Yorkshire which involved a lot of recces and photos. Most sites were remote from the A&E department and needed an ambulance transfer, which was a pain. Our best site was Leeds General Infirmary (LGI), which had a rooftop helipad. At some time in the past some forward-thinking administrator had had it built, not knowing when it might be used. The only functioning rooftop pad at that time in the UK was London HEMS. LGI was to be next but first, it had to pass inspection by the CAA, and it was my responsibility to make sure it would!

The porters at the hospital were all trained to CAA fire-fighting standard, and they serviced and monitored all of the equipment on the helipad. Incredibly dedicated people, they dropped what they were doing in order to man up the pad when we were inbound. The helipad was ready just before launch date. It was a blessing in disguise for us pilots, as in order to be at a safe single-engine landing weight, we had to keep the fuel to a minimum, while being able to cover the largest county in England! It was a difficult balancing act. Fuel at base gave us about one hour's flying. Say, twenty minutes to scene, twenty minutes to LGI, and we would be landing with twenty minutes fuel onboard, which was usually acceptable. Sometimes one paramedic would be left at scene in order to be at a safe landing weight. There were numerous airfields around the county where we could refuel, if required, and I set up a good working relationship with the military fields in the Vale of York, eventually getting landing fees waived, a policy which became standard at all military fields around the country thanks to us.

Mick and the paramedics begged, borrowed and stole equipment which was stashed in our portacabin. We were offered Ordinance Survey maps when we visited the flight planning section at RAF Linton-on-Ouse, so we took two of each for the whole of Yorkshire! There was a constant list of requirements to be filled when setting up the office, my head was definitely in a spin. With just one week to launch, PAS decided that I should do some shifts for West Yorkshire Police, flying their Bolkow from Carr Gate. While happy to help out, I still had so much to do. Mick was not at all happy and let PAS know, in no uncertain terms, but I was flying there on the 18th, 19th and 20th. It did give me a chance to really get to know our local engineer, Gareth Mayfield, who would be crucial to our success.

Yorkshire Air Ambulance went live, with the blessing of the CAA, on 25 October 2000. There was no great fanfare, the big PR push was to be the next day, the 26th. We did have a couple of flights on the 25th but no patients carried. However, back at base I discovered that our rotor brake had been sticking and the disc on the tail rotor drive shaft was warped. It needed replacing ASAP before the press launch the next day. I know military blokes can have a colourful vocabulary, but I think I learned a few new words from Gareth when I told him. He worked on it overnight and it would have been a very different start to YAA if he hadn't got it sorted.

On my days off in the early days, the flying was done by two MAS floater pilots, Clive Chandler and Stu Doyle, both ex-military and highly experienced. The paramedics warmed to them both and it enhanced the safety-first ethos I had hoped to instil.

The paramedics were, initially, from West Yorkshire Metropolitan Ambulance service (WYMAS) but were reinforced later on with colleagues from Tees, East and North Yorkshire Ambulance Service (TENYAS), and South Yorkshire Ambulance Service (SYAS). Many of them had long commutes to Leeds Airport in the early days. Mick had a job on his hands sorting out the roster!

Our tasking came from the control rooms of each of those Ambulance authorities. It took some time to educate them in what our capabilities were and to make sure that we were used effectively. The long-term goal was to have a dedicated air ambulance desk and that is just what has happened. In the early days we would quite often arrive after road ambulances were on scene, to be met with, 'Ere come 't 'elicopter 'eroes!' But road crews soon became used to us and appreciated the help we could bring to bear. Police units were another matter. West Yorkshire Police traffic units were concerned that our roadside landings would be a distraction to motorists. Mick and I were press-ganged into a meeting with senior officers where they told us that we were not to land unless a traffic unit was on scene and had picked a landing site for us. This was ridiculous and, in any case, as an Air Ambulance we were free to land and take-off anywhere, at our own discretion. The notion that we would delay attending to casualties until a copper decided we could land, was ridiculous and we told them so. The meeting did not end well but we knew our rights and responsibilities! No problems were encountered with South or North Yorkshire police, in fact they could not have been more helpful from the off.

So, the operational side of life was going well, and I was pleased with what we had accomplished in such a short time. The charity, on the other hand, was something of a nightmare! Initially, the funding of £1,000,000 annually was provided by the Automobile Association and I cannot praise or thank them highly enough. It was due to them that the Yorkshire Air Ambulance was started but, unfortunately, money like that attracts all kind of ne'er-do-wells. The charity chairman, to begin with, was Trevor Molton, Chief Executive of WYMAS, and his right-hand man was his Director of Finance, John Miners. Both of these clowns were to be convicted of fraud and imprisoned a few years later. They were taking advice regarding helicopter operations from a group described to me by my CAA Flight Ops inspector as 'The Yorkshire Mafia'. A group of amateur pilots and small-time helicopter operators who wanted to get their hands on the operation. Molton and Miners called a meeting with MAS's MD, Jeremy Awenat, at Multiflight, where I was present. They told him that MAS had to cut its contract rate by half, or they would pull the plug on YAA! Needless to say, this was outrageous and completely unacceptable. It was agreed that I would stay on to run things until they felt able to carry out their threat, as Jeremy was not changing the contract which reflected the going rate. I was distressed that my time in Yorkshire might be cut short.

A few months down the line, in April 2002, we took the helicopter to Northallerton for a charity event. The local MP was William Hague and I had the pleasure of taking him up for a spin. Upon landing, I was accosted by Molton and one of his helicopter friends, who asked me if I would leave my employment with MAS and take up direct employment under them, as Chief Pilot for an independent YAA. This would involve writing the Operations Manual and applying for an Air Operator's Certificate (AOC). I didn't like or trust Molton, so there was no way I would leave my employment with MAS. In any case, we had not been operating long enough for the CAA to consider granting an AOC and I told them so, again stating that I would stay on as Chief Pilot, running the operation until they had their own plans in place. This did not go down well, they had assumed that I would go along with their scheme, and, in fact, they had already submitted an application to the CAA through a small helicopter company using my name as Chief Pilot!

Yorkshire Air Ambulance

MAS Chief Pilot, Merrick Forsyth, got wind of this and rang me to ask what the hell I was up to. I was able to put him right and he informed the CAA of Molton's skullduggery. I was not at all happy and thought that my future with MAS might end up being a floater, with no fixed base when YAA did their own thing. Molton's next move was to put a half-page advertisement in Flight International magazine, at great expense, inviting applications for the position of Chief Pilot. Well, helicopters are a small world and the word had got round about what was happening, so there were few applicants. They ended up giving the post to a pilot from Finland who was qualified on the Bolkow but had never flown air ambulance and had never worked in the UK! It was to be his job to apply for the AOC and write the ops manual, while flying as my opposite number on my days off. They flew him and his family to Yorkshire and provided housing and a car, all at the charity's expense. MAS had to check him out on the Bolkow, then I had to line train him on the operation, which meant taking the air ambulance offline for three days. Three days with no air ambulance in Yorkshire! Ambulance staff had been told to refer to him as 'Chief Pilot' even while I was still in post.

Molton had also removed Mick Lindley from the unit, so I had no paramedic manager and had to run the rosters from three ambulance services myself plus arrange training for new applicants. I was not happy but kept up my smiling face when on shift, there was enough stress for paramedics to deal with without having a grumpy pilot. I loved, just *loved* the job we were doing. The AA money had stopped and there was a growing band of volunteers who were starting to raise money around Yorkshire. I knew when I took the job, that Yorkshire people would take us to heart and funds would not be a problem in the long run. It was starting to happen. But with what was happening, I needed to get away.

I started looking for employment elsewhere, even considering returning to the RAF. I had met my old mate Andy Pulford at the Wessex retirement bash at Odiham where he was now the Group Captain and had a chat over a beer in the mess. He was able to give me a contact in the MOD who could facilitate my rejoining as Specialist Aircrew. I didn't jump in straightaway though. It was obvious that our Finnish friend was getting nowhere with his paperwork and that the CAA would not consider him suitable to run an Air Ambulance. I had received informal complaints from Air Traffic that he was not talking to anyone on the radio outside controlled airspace, despite what I had taught him. It was important to keep nearby ATC units informed as to what we were doing as we might have needed urgent direct routing at short notice! For instance, one job I did to the North York Moors to attend a woodsman whose chainsaw has slipped and had half-severed his arm at the shoulder joint. We had to take him to York Infirmary and the direct route was straight through Linton-on-Ouse's zone. They were recovering 20 Tucanos at the time, following a practise formation for the Queen's golden jubilee. They requested that I route around their zone, but when the problem was explained they held off the Tucanos and cleared me direct to York. We always received this level of service from ATC when on a task and I didn't want to sour the atmosphere with any of them! The Finn was told in no uncertain terms what he should be doing. To cap it all he started to be aloof and detached from the paramedics on shift, not sharing the crew room at all and only communicating when a job came in.

Things were bad. Then an angel appeared named John Sutherland. No, not me, but a senior manager with WYMAS who shared my name. In 2003 he would visit us at the 'Sharp End' and keep us updated with what was happening regarding the charity. The police must have been catching up with Molton and Miners at this stage because John was able to tell us that they had been removed from the board, along with Molton's helicopter pal. The Finnish 'Chief Pilot' had been sacked and sent packing back to Finland with his family. Finally, I was able to get things running professionally and smoothly and Mick was re-appointed as unit manager which took a huge weight off my shoulders. Mick's boundless enthusiasm and passion for the job kept me on my toes. He wanted to start operating at night, just not possible in those days, but he wouldn't be happy until he received sound reasons why not. He wanted to have the capability to carry underslung loads to major incident sites. I couldn't knock him back on that one, so we fitted the sling hook and I started training the paramedics to give directions to the pilot while hanging out the door observing the load. They achieved a good standard, and I was always glad to hear their 'Up Gently'! We only used this facility on one occasion, a major incident exercise involving fire/police/ambulance, where we delivered a large inflatable triage tent. It was a great success but soon the fire service had purchased their own 'Rick-rack' style expandable unit. Mick was a driving force, and we would often have lively discussions about what we could and couldn't do!

In the early days we were lucky to have Dr Darren Walter as our medical director. He had had previous experience with London HEMS and was a passionate exponent of the use of helicopter air ambulances. Later, he moved on and Dr Alison Walker took over, an A&E consultant who overcame a fear of heights to become an integral member of the team. I want to name check all of the paramedics I worked with in Yorkshire; Mick, of course, Paul, Steve, Dave, Steve, Chris, Neil, Tracy, Julie, Graham, Graham, Neal, Simon, Pat, Paul, Steve, Chris, Debbie and Sammy. Each and every one of them had a profound effect on the life of those they dealt with. It was my privilege to be their 'Ambulance Driver' and see the amazing work they carried out, saving lives and helping others with compassion and understanding, in situations most of the public cannot envisage or understand. As we were generally attending first-line trauma incidents I was to witness some grisly sights. For instance, we attended a scene in North Yorkshire where a couple of lads high on cannabis had been walking on the main London-Newcastle railway line. Seeing a train coming, they ducked to one side, only to be hit by a train going the other way! Both alive, but nasty injuries. As the paramedics treated them a fire officer handed me an arm, severed just above the elbow. I put it in a plastic bag and placed it in the rear of the Bolkow. We took the worst injured patient to St James hospital in Middlesbrough where they also amputated a leg. It was not possible to re-attach the arm, but the lad survived!

I mentioned the need to maintain a good lookout, but I was lapse myself one day, nearly causing a collision. We were returning to Leeds on a fine Sunday afternoon, flying at 3,000 feet and talking to Church Fenton radar, who had no traffic on their screen. We were above Breighton airfield when Steve Morell in the seat behind me shouted 'Go down'! My eyeline to the right was level with the top door frame but I ducked down, to see a glider coming at us, same height and on a collision course! Rules of the Air gave him right of way, it was my responsibility to look that way. I had been lulled into a false sense of security by imagining that radar would be seeing everything, which they weren't, as some gliders have a poor radar return. I dropped the collective and pushed so hard on the cyclic that I fooled the flight controls into thinking that they had jammed, so the secondary hydraulic system came online. We had negative G for a split second so loose maps and equipment floated up to the roof and we were forced up in our straps as the nose went forward. The Bolkow was one of only a few helicopters which would take such a manoeuvre. I was worried that it was too late and was waiting for the tail rotor to hit. It didn't! We regained straight and level and I declared an air miss to the radar controller. The official report, published later, praised my quick reactions but castigated me, quite rightly, for my poor lookout. When there is an obstruction to your eyeline you must move your head to get a better view. I hadn't, and it was Steve leaning forward to grab a map which had lowered his head below the door frame, giving him sight of the glider. If he hadn't done that at just that moment, I reckon we would have collided and crashed.

For the third anniversary of YAA it was arranged to have a publicity shoot at Breighton, flying in formation with the Hurricane WW2 fighter based there. Our helicopter's full title was Messerschmitt-Bolkow-Blohm Bo 105, so, in effect, we had a Hurricane and Messerschmitt airborne over Yorkshire. We flew over there, and I met up with Brian Brown, the Hurricane pilot and a renowned warbird display pilot. We went over a comprehensive briefing about what we would do, then got into our respective aircraft and started up. There were TV crews and newspaper reporters in attendance filming and

Yorkshire Air Ambulance

A Hurricane and a Messerschmitt in formation over Yorkshire.

photographing everything. I was airborne first, as it was easier for Brian to catch me up! We flew over the airfield in formation, then changed for me to formate on the Hurricane. It was one of the most amazing personal experiences I had had, I was so excited to be flying so close to this beautiful classic aircraft. It was over too soon, and I returned to land, while Brian gave the news crews a brief display. It was a very successful day.

I would undertake any task to gain publicity and when we were approached by Yorkshire TV to be part of their 'St Jimmys' programme it was too good to miss. It was a fly-on-the-wall series documenting the work of staff at St James hospital in Leeds, a place where we took many patients. They wanted me to fly a priest who was a member of their staff to give him an appreciation of the experience that some of his patients had had. No problem and great publicity. As the day approached, I received a phone call from Merrick Forsyth, MAS Chief Pilot, who was not happy. He had been told that we were planning to fly a priest to serious accidents to administer the last rites if needed! I was able to put him right on that and he liked the actual truth of what we were doing. I was unable to trace who had told him the story. But I have my suspicions Gareth?

I had another close call one day when landing in a farmer's field between the farm and an outbuilding. We were in a high hover, descending to land when Sammy Wills, in the rear seat, called 'Up, up, up'! There was a thin telephone wire stretched across the field from one building to the other. It was under the tail boom, just behind the fuselage, and the boom was actually depressing it! Had it snapped, it could have whipped into the main or tail rotor, which would not have been a good thing. I complied with Sammy's directions immediately and disaster was averted. Again, due to diligence by a crewmember.

Into our fourth year of operation and things were running smoothly. We started a week-long trial with a second helicopter based at Sheffield airport, on lease from MAS. It was a great success, of course, Yorkshire is the biggest county in England and needs two helicopters. The funding was not yet available to make it a permanent arrangement, but it was obvious that it would be there in the future. It's here that I must make an apology to Richard Hammond. I had said to Mick that what we needed was a high-profile celebrity to have a mishap in Yorkshire and be carried by us in order to save their life. And so it was for poor Richard, suffering a crash on the runway at Elvington a couple of years later when he was testing a jet-powered dragster. The publicity increased funds rapidly after that. But I do feel bad for having put that out to the universe.

I now had Steve Beaumont as my back-to-back and a regular stand-in pilot was Pete Barnes, a contract pilot working as a floater for PAS/MAS. Pete was a larger-than-life character, a good pilot who had flown an Explorer in the Bond movie *Die Another Day*. He was not ex-military but had gained his licence through working in the civilian world. I'm sure I didn't need to, but I felt it necessary to remind him that we weren't paid to go flying, we earned our wages by saying 'No' when conditions weren't suitable. Pete was a likeable character who got on well with the paramedics. He was to die in a crash in central London a few years later.

In 2004 I received a phone call, from my old mate John Tickner (of Fat Geordie Bastard fame) in Sussex. The helicopter unit there was leaving the PAS contract and gaining its own Operator's Certificate, planning to employ pilots directly. He kindly asked me if I would consider returning there to be one of those pilots. It was a hard decision to make, Yorkshire Air Ambulance was my baby and was now growing into a successful enterprise with another helicopter on the horizon and gaining its own AOC. But I knew Steve Beaumont would gladly take it on and the charity was now running smoothly, so I took the decision to leave. I was thinking of my future pension and being employed directly by the police in Sussex would be a good option. Plus, Debbie and I both had family there. So, we were leaving. The paramedics arranged a treat for me before going, a flight with Brian Brown in a Bucker Jungmann biplane (the Luftwaffe equivalent of the Tiger Moth), from Breighton airfield. It was a memorable day; Brian gave me free rein with the old aeroplane, and I looped and rolled until I was remembering those queasy feelings from Jet Provost days! Brian was to die in an air display crash.

Chapter 10

Back to the Future

A nd so, I returned to Sussex in 2004, to the Explorer, to my old unit and my old friends, plus a few new faces. I fully expected to see out my career there and enjoy the benefits of direct employment with the Police, which was on the cards. It was good to be back on the Explorer and it was a busy time with the usual mix of police and ambulance work up to the close of the year. Then in January I received an email from my Aussie mate in Oman, Phil Stevens, telling me that he was leaving there and that I should apply to return to the Royal Flight. The job was being advertised in *Flight* magazine, but I wasn't looking to move and hadn't seen it! I didn't think for one second that I would be welcomed back after my ignominious departure, but Phil was insistent that, if I applied, I would be considered. I didn't reply to the advertisement but decided to write directly to the Commander of Royal Flight, a post now filled by Mohammed Hamdan, who had been deputy when I left. I asked if my punishment in exile for 12 years was complete and wondered if he would consider me for the vacancy. If not, I would understand of course, and asked him to pass my regards to the blokes. But I would be delighted if I could be considered suitable.

The next that I heard was an invitation to an interview at Gatwick! I went along to meet the chief helicopter pilot, Abdullah Obaidani, plus the head of admin and a Royal Guard officer. Abdullah had joined RF from the Royal Air Force of Oman (RAFO, previously SOAF) and Omanisation was gaining pace. The interview went well, and I awaited the result which would take a few weeks. Then, in March, the news came, the job was mine! I was almost in disbelief but happy to be returning. I then had to break the news to Cliff and Ian that, despite telling them that I had come back to Sussex to stay, I had now accepted a job offer at another of my old units.

Debbie and I were scheduled to leave for Oman in August. My flying continued up to then, the most notable incident being a bird strike in May. A bloody big buzzard which was stooging around North of Lancing College at 500 feet, just as I was approaching Shoreham airfield from that direction. Now, a buzzard rules the sky and doesn't expect to have to move for anyone. I didn't see it until the last second, just started to pull up but it hit the chin window, bang! Smashed through onto my shins and ended up on top of my feet on the pedals, very dead. Feathers filled the cockpit. I pushed out a 'Pan' call and landed in a field, straight ahead. I rang the engineers at

Back to the Future

Following a collision with a buzzard.

PAS in Gloucester and, joining the digital age for the first time, used my phone to send pictures of the damage. It was confined to the smashed Perspex and bruises on my legs! The crew were collected by vehicle, and I flew the helicopter for one mile back to the hangar for repair. The next day I drove to Gloucester to collect the company spare, a Bolkow which we had to put up with for the next three weeks while repairs were made. The incident was picked up by the media and there was a report in the Brighton Argus, along with a picture of me in front of the helicopter, holding the dead buzzard. Then I was invited to the BBC Sussex studio for a chat on the breakfast show, sanctioned by Cliff, of course! The BBC wanted to do an item covering my career, but the Royal Flight wouldn't approve it.

My next step back in time was returning to Oman in August 2005. Debbie was with me of course and we were starting out on a thirteen-year stint living as expatriates. Royal Flight had changed greatly since my departure twelve years previously. Omanisation was in full flow with many of the locals now in charge. Najeeb and Omar had moved across to us from the ROP, as two of the most experienced Omani pilots, plus a handful of ex-RAFO (previously SOAF) pilots. There were expats as well, and a much more cosmopolitan bunch than previously. Pilots from UK, USA, Australia, Ireland, France and Belgium would come and go during my time there.

The Helicopter fleet comprised the same Pumas and Super Pumas as when I had left, although plans were well advanced to replace them. I enjoyed flying them again, like greeting old friends! I slipped easily into the old routine of training trips, deployments to the interior when HM went camping, spending time in Salalah and Sohar with just a couple of VIP trips when I flew the Dutch and South Korean prime ministers in 2006.

The 330J Pumas used in the trooping role were replaced in 2006 with the military version of the single-engined Eurocopter Squirrel, the Fennec. It was wholly unsuited to the task, but the story goes that a senior member of the Royal Guard had liked the look of it at the Dubai Airshow and insisted that the Royal Flight should purchase them. Rumours of brown envelopes changing hands were just rumours. Payload was minimal, exacerbated by the fact that it was crewed with two pilots at the behest of HM. It was unable to escort the Super Pumas on flying tasks as it couldn't keep up. It was flown mainly by the Omanis to begin with. I and the other older expats remained on the larger helicopters. As new expats joined Royal Flight they were put to work on the Fennec, joined by a new cadre of ab-initio trainees moved to Royal Flight from the Royal Air Force of Oman (RAFO Previously known as SOAF). Operating these smaller helicopters was seen as a stepping-stone to employment on the VIP helicopters. I must say that the Fennec crews became very slick at escorting road vehicles when HM was on the move. It was impressive hearing the coordinated movements of helicopters around the convoy, especially on night moves. Oh yes, most road convoys were now at night, the Fennecs down low escorting the vehicles and scouting the road, the VIP helicopters up high, available if needed, although nobody seemed to have got the message to the Royal Guard that we would probably not be able to land, at night, in the middle of nowhere! General Harcort had always made sure that HM's moves were done in daylight, but he was long gone.

Sad news came from England in December 2006 about the crash of a Bond Dauphin. One of the pilots was my mate Steve Potton, who had been copilot for me when we flew Cecil Parkinson from Blackpool Airport, out to the Irish Sea gas field. Steve was promoted to Chief Pilot at Blackpool and was checking out a new copilot, flying to that same field, on the night they crashed into the sea approaching a rig. No survivors.

Up Gently

Our new helicopter type arrived in January 2007, the EC225. It was the ultimate development of the Super Puma, now with electronic engine control (FADEC) and a fully integrated autopilot and avionics suite. The cockpit layout was very similar to Airbus fixed-wing designs as we were told by our senior training captain, Jerry Smith—ex-RAF of course, some standards had to be maintained—who had been flying Airbus 340s before coming to Oman. With uprated engines and a higher maximum weight, what could go wrong? Converting to these helicopters required a completely different approach to cockpit management. Most functions were accessed by pressing buttons or twiddling knobs. Apart from lifting into the hover, or landing on from the hover, piloting skills were not required, just the ability to program the Flight Management System (FMS) and select the appropriate autopilot mode. On one of my conversion trips we were returning to Muscat. When flying downwind to land I disconnected the automatics and put my hands on the controls to fly around to the landing point. My French instructor, Pierre, became quite agitated 'Non! Use the automatic functions until you are closer to landing!' So, I engaged the autopilot modes, took my right hand off the cyclic and stuffed it into my flying suit breast. 'OK, I will be like Napoleon!' By selecting headings, heights and speeds by twiddling knobs with my left hand, I brought us down to the landing point. By double-clicking the top left button on the cyclic (much like using a mouse) the helicopter came to a hover with no manual input at all. Then by squeezing down the cyclic with my left hand, we came down to the ground, where I again disconnected the autopilot. No coordination required!

With the 225 now on my licence I took another step into the past when I was seconded to Bristow helicopters in Aberdeen for one month in 2007. The idea was to build up some hours on the new type before being unleashed upon VVIP passengers. I was checked out by Captain White, Senior Training Pilot, who had been a junior copilot flying with me at Bond Helicopters 20 years previously. The boy done good! I then settled into the routine flying back and forwards to the rigs. The 225 was a major improvement on the Super Puma, reducing the cockpit workload considerably.

Back to Oman and back to training and following the Sultan around the country, plus the occasional visiting VIP. One trip of note was flying the US Secretary of State for the Middle East, accompanied by the US Ambassador and the Omani Foreign Minister. Having started the first engine and got the rotors spinning, the second engine would not respond. The only solution was to shut down again, switch off the battery, and then start again. Very much like Control/Alt/Delete on your computer! I apologised to our guests and explained the situation. They understood completely, especially the 'reset' requirement. Both engines behaved themselves and started nicely on the second attempt, much to my relief.

Up Gently

September 2007 brought more bad news from England. Brian Brown, the display pilot from Yorkshire, who had flown a Hurricane in formation with my YAA Bolkow and also took me up in the Bucker Jungman, had crashed and died in the Hurricane during a display at Shoreham Airport. A terrible shock but reinforcing the fact that aviation is a dangerous business and no respecter of experience and ability!

2008 saw the Sultan off on a summer cruise so we decamped onto the *Fulk Al Salamah* and followed him around the Mediterranean although there was no helicopter flying on the whole trip. Debbie was able to join me for a break in Palermo and Rome.

2009 began with a visit to Oman by the Dutch Prince of Orange and his beautiful wife, Princess Maxima. We collected them from the Al Bustan Hotel and flew them to meet the Sultan at Bait Al Barka. Unfortunately, the Oman football team were playing the final of the Gulf Cup and the match had gone to extra time. HM and his boys were watching it so the meeting with the royal visitors was delayed! Oman eventually won the game, and the audience went ahead. We flew them back to the hotel later and the prince popped up to the cockpit for a chat. A pilot himself, he showed a great interest in the 225 and we enjoyed his company.

My major achievement for that year was procuring flight planning software for the 225. Pete Rowlinson, previously a colleague pilot in Sussex, was now running a computing company,

'Easyweigh', with software tailored to individual flight operations and companies. I had used his services in both Sussex and Yorkshire, so I was keen to get it for Royal Flight. As it was, we had to consult eleven graphs and tables in the Flight Manual, before each flight. With Easyweigh installed on laptops, we could click crewmembers/ passengers/ freight/ fuel, then input the weather conditions and it produced all of the necessary performance figures in seconds. I also enjoyed a week back in the UK meeting old friends, collecting the software and being briefed by Pete.

Flying time was very limited, a lot of time was spent on standby. I was averaging 80 hours per year and that was the case in 2010 and 2011. 2010 was the last year in which there was a major desert convoy by HM, on a move north from Salalah. Unusually, he flew by helicopter on one of the moves. He had been flying less and less each year and his health was deteriorating.

I had a few VIP flights over the next few years. The first was in January 2012, transporting Queen Beatrice of the Netherlands, along with her son and his wife. We were to collect her at the Al Bustan Hotel, take her and her entourage to the Royal Dutch Shell facility at the new Sohar port, then on to the historic Fort at Nakhl before returning her to the hotel. I was designated task leader for the trip, flying in the lead helicopter with Thierry Pejon, a French ex-special forces pilot. There were six helicopters in the formation. Two RF VIP 225s, one RF trooping 225 full of

Royal Guard soldiers, two RAFO NH90s for staff/protocol etc, and one ROP AW189 in the medevac role with doctors and nurses on board. I had my work cut out briefing everyone on who was doing what, where and when! Everything went smoothly and, on return to the hotel, the Queen thanked us personally by the helicopter. A wonderful lady.

We had had to stop all flying for a while in 2009 following a North Sea Super Puma crash in April, where the rotor head detached from the gearbox and it plunged into the sea, killing all on board. Gearbox modifications had supposedly solved the problem but during 2012 two 225s had to ditch into the North Sea, both with gearbox lubrication problems. Everybody survived but things were not good with the helicopter's reputation! Following extensive modifications, we were eventually allowed to operate again, but, to nobody's surprise, use of maximum torque all the time was stopped, and cruise speed subsequently reduced by a few knots. It made little difference but obviously saved wear on the gearbox!

January 2013 brought the awful news of another friend crashing and dying. Pete Barnes, the flamboyant character who had been flying for me at Yorkshire Air Ambulance, was flying along the Thames in London in marginal weather. He decided to turn back but made contact with a crane on top of a tower block at Vauxhall. On plummeting to the ground, he unfortunately killed an innocent pedestrian.

Back to the Future

We were still not cleared to fly VIP passengers when Charles and Camilla visited Oman in March 2013 and they had the ignominy of having to fly in a ROP helicopter for a visit to Nizwa. We did fly but only carrying minor staff and Royal Guard. Later in 2013 the 225 had a clean bill of health and we had the pleasure of taking King Abdullah of Jordan from Muscat Airport to Wattayah Stadium in the capital, where HM was waiting to meet him. He was due to travel by road, but his flight had been delayed. We always manned up the helicopters for VIP arrivals, just in case, although we were very rarely used. But this was one of those rare occasions. Bodyguards and protocol personnel running around like mad, shouting at us to get ready. I was copilot, so standing by the cabin door, saluting the King as he walked over from his aircraft, then shutting the door after he was onboard. A quick start, priority from air traffic, then we were on our way, only ten minutes to the stadium. When we landed, a quick shutdown, climb out and doors open. Royal guards rushed over to escort the King to meet HM as he was running late. But he wouldn't have it. He pushed back and came over to me and Saud, the crewman, to shake our hands and thank us. A true Gentleman.

The Sultan's health was deteriorating, and he moved to a medical facility in Germany in 2014, not returning until March 2015.

In the meantime, our training and tasking continued. Prince Harry arrived in Oman in November 2014, and I was tasked to collect him from the Al Bustan Hotel and fly him to Nizwa, where he was visiting the Fort and meeting schoolchildren and local dignitaries. Nasser Kalbani was my copilot. An experienced ex-RAFO pilot, he was a thorough professional and a pleasure to fly with. He had recently been promoted to be Najeeb's deputy as Chief Pilot, deservedly so. The trip went well, then a curve ball was thrown at us when our VIPs came onboard at Nizwa. Harry's ADC came to the cockpit and told us that the prince would like to see the ground route taken up the mountainside by the SAS for a famous assault on Saiq plateau. He was clutching a small-scale ordnance survey map with the route pencilled on. Let me say at this point that we had sophisticated navigation equipment, GPS, tied into the autopilot and a moving-map display, but we had to forget all of this and go back to basic eyeball map reading. I was glad that I was the handling pilot as the navigation duty fell to Nasser! He made a superb job of it, we hover-taxied up the mountainside, putting the route on our right-hand side, the side where Harry was sitting, ending up landing on the strip at Saiq army base. The VIPs deplaned for a short tour around the base, before getting back on board for the trip back to Muscat and a landing at the main army base there. Nasser jumped out to open the cabin door and salute our guests. But before they left Harry said thank you to me sat in the cockpit. I told him that he could tell his brother that he'd been flown around Oman by an ex-22 Sqn bloke who had also flown

Back to the Future

Air Ambulance! He laughed. He was my last VIP passenger.

Into 2015 and a major task. Najeeb wanted me to fly a 225 all the way to Stavanger in Norway, where it was due a deep service to be carried out by Helikopter Service there. I was crewed up with Kevin Rutherford, a highly experienced ex-Royal Navy pilot who had joined Royal Flight initially on the Fennec, but had recently gained his command on the 225. Our third pilot was Ahmed Rashidi, a young Omani, ex-RAFO, who had also been on the Fennec but was now a first officer on the 225. With our crewman and engineers there were seven of us making the trip. Some major planning was required along with visas and diplomatic clearances.

Kev was a wizard with submitting ICAO flight plans, so I was very happy to delegate those to him! The route went initially to Doha in Qatar for our first night stop. The next day was spent crossing Saudi Arabia with refuels at Riyadh and Medina. None of us wanted the hassle of a night in Saudi! So, we continued to Luxor in Egypt. We had a day off there and I organised a trip to the Valley of the Kings. I had been given a large cash kitty, to be used for gratuities mainly but, with a bit of creative accounting, to pay for some crew enjoyment! Tourism in Egypt had collapsed after some crazed gunmen had carried out attacks, so the guides were happy to see us. Luxor Airport was empty.

From there we flew to Cyprus after a refuel in Alexandria. Next day to Kalamata in Greece for fuel, then to Lamezia on the 'toe' of Italy, where we enjoyed a fantastic meal at a wonderful Italian restaurant where the locals really made us feel welcome. On to Marseille with a refuel on Corsica. Two nights there and then on to Bordeaux. We were taking the long way around France because it was late February, and we were flying on Visual Flight Rules (VFR) meaning we couldn't fly in cloud due to icing. Kevin and Ahmed were flying the afternoon leg from Bordeaux to Le Touquet when the weather deteriorated, and Kevin made the wise decision to turn back. So, a night stop in Bordeaux, then on to Le Touquet the next day where we had the hotel to ourselves and another great night out at a French restaurant. My cash fund was dwindling fast, but I had been generously tipping refuellers/handling agents/ security/hotel concierges along the route as briefed by Najeeb. After all, we were the Royal Flight of Oman. The final day saw us going to Esbjerg in Denmark for fuel before making our triumphant arrival into Stavanger. Job done!

For my 60th birthday in December Najeeb gave me a present. Shift 40 tonnes of underslung loads for building work at Jalali Palace. I had another senior Omani, Riyadh, as my copilot. It was great to be doing some real helicopter work, not just training or doing gentle VIP trips. The 225 made short work of it, loads of power and great to fly with a load attached.

I was expecting to work in Oman through 2019 and had been assured of it by Abdullah Obaidani, but fate had a different idea.

Back to the Future

The author's sixtieth birthday in Oman.

Epilogue

D ebbie and I had bought a house in Cabo San Lucas, Mexico, ready for my future retirement in 2020. We had been renting it out as a holiday let but spending our leave periods there. April 2016 was one of those visits. Lori, the wife of our realtor, was visiting us for afternoon tea when she mentioned that her friend's husband was a helicopter pilot who had also retired to Cabo. I was intrigued. She said that he was considering starting a tourist helicopter business. I told her that I would love to meet him, so she phoned her friend, Christina, and a meeting was agreed for lunchtime the next day. The gentleman's name was Patrick Corr. He had built up the largest helicopter training school in America before selling it to Bristow Helicopters and retiring on the proceeds. I was excited to hear what his plans were and to meet up with him. The next day, 29 April, dawned with the terrible news of another 225 crashing in Norway. Once again, the rotors had detached from the gearbox, and they had dropped like a stone from 2,000 feet.

Epilogue

It was a sobering topic to start our conversation. I got on well with Patrick and Christina immediately and was fascinated with his plans to introduce an EC130 for tourist flying and possibly building a dedicated heliport closer to the town centre. My interest was increased by the realisation that my flying in Oman was probably about to end with the grounding of all 225s. Lunch ended with an agreement that Patrick was keen that I should be involved in the future. I promised to keep in touch.

We returned to Oman and as expected, the 225s were grounded indefinitely. It was a blessing for me as in the next few months Debbie needed major surgery in Bangkok and then my mother passed away in August and I was shuttling from Thailand to UK and back to Oman. After that my priority was to gain my American licence to be able to fly in Cabo. This was done with a conversion of my Omani ATPL to a US ATP which involved studying for the ground exams and completing a flight test on a US registered helicopter. I opted to go to Florida to fly a Robinson R44, my first piston-engined helicopter. I had never imagined that, at age 60, I would be cramming for exams and learning to operate a completely new type! It was a requirement to have 10 hours on the R44 before gaining the licence, so I needed a couple of weeks with an instructor. The unfortunate individual was Ryan Walker, an ex-US Marine who was just fantastic at helping this geriatric Brit pilot find a way through the labyrinth of FAA regulations and in encouraging me to lose my bad habits from years of flying. It had to be the R44, Ryan and I could have squeezed in to an R22, but we would have had about 5 minutes fuel at max weight!

Florida weather meant that we could fly with the doors off, which also meant that I had to be diligent with maps/charts/checklists so they didn't fly out of the cockpit. The cockpit itself was very cramped of course, with minimal instrumentation. There is only one cyclic stick on Robinsons, located centrally between the two front seats with a hinged 'Y' handle on top to allow either pilot to use it. The radios and navaids were controlled from a Garmin GPS display unhelpfully located low down behind the cyclic stick. For the ATP test instrument flying was included although the R44 was not cleared for actual IFR flight, only training and tests where the handling pilot (me) wore goggles to only show the instrument panel. When required, I could say 'Autopilot' to Ryan and he would hold it straight and level while I retuned and planned procedures.

I didn't adapt to it quickly and Ryan was very patient going over the requirements. General handling was fine but it's not a helicopter I enjoyed flying. Ryan paid me the compliment of saying that at least he didn't think I was trying to kill him, as some previous students had! Ground exams passed, FAA class one medical obtained with a local doctor, then the day for the flight test arrived. My examiner was a Vietnam Vet, Dave Evans, so even older than me. I got on very well with him and passed the test despite my fumblings with the Garmin.

Epilogue

With Ryan Walker, an ex-US Marine instructor.

Back to Oman for Christmas and the confirmation that my contract would not be renewed, along with two other expat pilots who were over-60. I had been expecting another three years of wages to build up my retirement fund but that was gone. We arranged our resident visas and prepared to leave for Mexico in July. Patrick informed me that the EC130 would be there by then. In the meantime, I cadged rides in the Fennecs as often as I could. The Fennec had exactly the same engine and gearbox as the EC130, and the cockpit layout was very similar, so it proved invaluable. Plus, I was flying from the left-hand seat which was actually the captain's seat on the EC130 which had a wider cabin, making it easier to load and offload tourists from the right.

A charter came up in the first week we were there. Patrick asked me to accompany him to see how things worked. It was an eye-opener! We were to fly the American comedienne Jessica Williams and her partner, collecting them at

Up Gently

San Jose del Cabo airfield, flying north to La Paz airfield to refuel, then delivering her to Ciudad Constitution airfield up the Baja peninsula. They were being collected by vehicle to take them to a boat on the west coast. We were not allowed to land at the port. In fact, the authorities would not allow us to land anywhere other than an airfield with a runway. It would have made more sense for the poor woman to have chartered a small fixed-wing, much as we enjoyed her company! At each airfield they demanded to see *all* of the aircraft documents plus the pilots' licences. Then a full ICAO flight plan had to be filed for each leg, airfield to airfield. I had never seen such bureaucracy. It was the norm for the rest of my flights from Cabo. However, I think that if brown envelopes had been offered then the Mexicans might have been more flexible in their attitude. But Patrick, quite rightly, was not going to play those games. It did severely curtail our operation, most resorts and high-end beach rentals had plenty of space for a helicopter to land. But we were stuck with operating only from airfields and the few flights I did do all took off from Cabo, half an hour's sightseeing, then landed back at Cabo. The only USP was the novelty of flying in a helicopter.

After a few months Debbie's health started to deteriorate and it was obvious that Cabo was not the place to be for her. We put our house on the market and made plans to return to the UK.

My last ever flight was in March 2018, taking a lovely retired German couple for a spin towards

Flying the Eurocopter EC130.

San Jose, then along the coast towards the famous Cabo arch, before returning to make my smoothest touchdown outside the hangar. Job done and I have a lump in my throat even as I type this.

I thank Patrick for giving me the chance to extend my flying for another year. It was obvious that there was no money to be made there and he wound up the operation shortly afterwards.

Forty years of helicopter flying had, finally, come to an end.

The author at the age of sixty, close to the end of his service with the Royal Flight of Oman.

SunRise

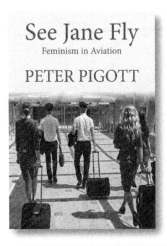

See Jane Fly
Feminism in Aviation

PETER PIGOTT

Sky Talk

Stories from flying's Golden Age

Philip Hogge

The Golden Age of Flying Boats

Peter Pigott

THE CONSTELLATION
Lockheed's Graceful Masterpiece

Alexander Clifton

www.sunpub.info

Printed in Great Britain
by Amazon

36323028R00106